A DREAM THAT INTERPRETS ITSELF

A DREAM THAT INTERPRETS ITSELF

Otto Rank

Edited by Robert Kramer

Translated by Gregory C. Richter

KARNAC
firing the mind

First published in German in 1910 as "Ein Traum, der sich selbst deutet" in the journal *Jahrbuch für psychoanalytische und psychopathologische Forschungen, 2*(2): 465–540.

First published in English in 2024 by
Karnac Books Limited
62 Bucknell Road
Bicester
Oxfordshire OX26 2DS

British Library Cataloguing in Publication Data

A C.I.P. for this book is available from the British Library

ISBN-13: 978-1-80013-205-4

Typeset by Medlar Publishing Solutions Pvt Ltd, India

www.firingthemind.com

Contents

About the author

Otto Rank was an Austrian psychoanalyst, writer, and philosopher. Freud considered Rank to be the most brilliant of his disciples. With access to the master's most intimate thoughts and feelings, Rank contributed two chapters to *The Interpretation of Dreams* in 1914. His name would appear below Freud's on the title page for the next fifteen years.

In the wake of Freud's rage against the preoedipal thesis of *The Trauma of Birth* (1924), which proposed the heresy that mothers are just as powerful as fathers, those Rank had trained as analysts in Vienna were required to be re-analysed by Freudians in order to retain their credentials. Co-creator of the psychoanalytic movement with Freud, Rank was now anathema. His enemies in the inner circle, especially Ernest Jones, "fell on him like dogs," said Helene Deutsch, an early analyst.

For almost a century, Rank has been vilified, ignored, or simply forgotten by the psychoanalytic establishment. But with the publication in 1973 of Ernest Becker's Pulitzer-Prize-winning *The Denial of Death*, Rank's fortunes began to change dramatically. Single-handedly, Becker brought Rank back from the dead, making a powerful case that Rank was the most brilliant mind in Freud's circle, with more insight into human nature than even the master himself.

If the twentieth century was Freud's, the twenty-first century, as Becker predicted fifty years ago, is shaping up to be that of Rank, "the brooding genius waiting in the wings," according to Irvin Yalom.

About the editor

Robert Kramer, PhD, is Visiting Professor of Psychology at Eötvös Loránd University (ELTE) in Budapest. At ELTE, he teaches Rankian psychotherapy to MA and PhD students. During Spring 2022, he was Professor of Psychoanalysis at ELTE, only the second person in Hungary to hold this title. The first was Sándor Ferenczi.

In addition to teaching at ELTE, he is now designing a leadership development program for the Leadership Academy of the Democracy Institute of Central European University in Budapest. Based on Rank's will therapy, the program will address the leadership needs of Central and Eastern European national and local leaders; politicians; policy experts in public administration and think tanks; and civil society activists who are working to promote democratic change. Concurrently, he is doing the same for Western European leaders at the Instituto Superior de Ciências Sociais e Políticas at the University of Lisbon.

During the academic year 2015–2016, he was the inaugural International Chair of Public Leadership at the National University of Public Service in Budapest, Hungary. In 2016, he resigned his chair due to the corruption of the Orbán regime.

He has published in *The Los Angeles Review of Books*, *The Times of Israel* (Tel Aviv), and *The New European* (London). He also writes reviews of forthcoming books for *Publishers Weekly* (New York). He edited and introduced Otto Rank's *A Psychology of Difference: The American Lectures* (Princeton University Press, 1996) and co-edited, with E. J. Lieberman, *The Letters of Sigmund Freud and Otto Rank: Inside Psychoanalysis* (Johns Hopkins University Press, 2012). In 2022, he published *The Birth of Relationship Therapy: Carl Rogers Meets Otto Rank* (Psychosozial Press). In 2024, Oxford University Press will publish his book *Otto Rank and the Creation of Modern Psychotherapy*. In 2025, he will edit, introduce, and publish a new translation of Rank's *Will Therapy* for Leuven University Press.

His peer-reviewed articles have appeared in the US, the UK, and, in translation, in Austria, Canada, China, France, Germany, Hungary, Lithuania, the Netherlands, and Spain. His latest, 'Discovering the Existential Unconscious: Rollo May Encounters Otto Rank' (*The Humanistic Psychologist*, March 2023), was published in translation in Chinese and Russian, and is now being translated into Greek, Turkish, and Hungarian. He serves on the editorial board of the *Journal of Humanistic Psychology* (US), founded by Abraham Maslow, and was book review editor of the *Journal of Organizational Change Management* (UK) for over a decade.

Before he moved to Budapest, he was Director of Executive Education for US government leaders at American University (AU)'s School of Public Affairs in Washington, DC. In 2002, he created "Transformative Action Learning," a Rankian leader development process and introduced it into the executive leadership curriculum at AU and at other universities around the world. In 2002, he received the Outstanding Teacher Award at AU. In 2004, he won the Curriculum Innovation Award of the American Society for Public Administration. From 2002 to 2004, he was an elected member of the Board of Directors of the Organizational Behavior Teaching Society for Management Educators, a group of 650 professors in leadership and management education worldwide.

He has lectured on Rank at the 3rd World Congress on Existential Psychology in Athens; Bar Ilan University in Tel Aviv; Sigmund Freud University in Vienna; Corvinus University of Budapest; Central European University (Budapest); George Washington University

(Washington, DC); American University (Washington, DC); the American Psychological Association; the International Psychoanalytical Association (Prague); the Freud Museum in Vienna; University of Lancaster (UK); University of Athens Medical School in Greece; the International Institute of Existential and Humanistic Psychology in Beijing; the Department of Psychiatry at the Universities of Pisa and Florence (Italy); the Colloquium on Intellectual History of European Psychology, La Maison des Sciences de l'Homme (Paris); the William Alanson White Institute in New York; the Indiana Society for Psychoanalytic Thought in Indianapolis; the Existential-Humanistic Institute in San Francisco; and the University of Pennsylvania School of Social Work in Philadelphia.

For twenty-five years, he served in progressively senior positions in the US government, including two years on Vice-President Al Gore's task force to reinvent the federal government and one year as Director of the Innovation University at the US Employment and Training Administration, with a budget of 10 billion dollars and over 1,000 employees. In 1999, he was selected by the US State Department to be a Fulbright Professor in Hungary, and taught leadership and organization development at Eötvös Loránd University in Budapest. He speaks Hungarian.

Applying Otto Rank's approach to will therapy, he has consulted on leader development to corporate, government, and civil society organizations around the world. Clients include Pfizer Corporation; Boeing Corporation; the World Bank; the European Commission in Brussels and Luxembourg; the European Environmental Agency in Copenhagen; the Prime Minister's Office in Tallinn, Estonia; the National Research University's Higher School of Economics in Moscow and St. Petersburg; the Moscow State University of Pedagogy; the University of Haifa; the Philippine Academy of Development; a large number of agencies of the US Government, including the intelligence community; and the Department of Human Services in the City of Alexandria in the US.

He holds a PhD in leadership, with a specialization in the intellectual history of psychoanalysis, from the George Washington University School of Business and Public Management in Washington, DC.

About the translator

Gregory C. Richter (PhD in Linguistics, University of California San Diego, 1982) taught German and Linguistics at Truman State University, Missouri, from 1983 to 2022. He maintains interests in formal linguistics and in translation theory. His publications include numerous translations from German, and centre on Viennese psychoanalysis. He has produced new renderings of *Beyond the Pleasure Principle* (2011), *The Future of an Illusion* (2012), and *Civilization and its Discontents* (2015) by Sigmund Freud, all at Broadview Press. He has also produced translations of Otto Rank's *The Incest Theme in Literature and Legend* (1992), *Psychology and the Soul* (1998, with E. James Lieberman), and *The Myth of the Birth of the Hero* (2004, with E. James Lieberman), all at Johns Hopkins University Press. More recently, he served as translator for *The Letters of Sigmund Freud and Otto Rank: Inside Psychoanalysis* (2011, edited by E. James Lieberman and Robert Kramer), Johns Hopkins University Press. Other publications include translations of works in French and Chinese. In the past few years, he has also served as copy editor for two presses—Ex Ophidia Press and Plain Wrapper Press Redux.

Introduction

Robert Kramer

Otto Rank was Sigmund Freud's closest colleague in Vienna during the formative years of psychoanalysis, from 1906 until 1926. In 1907, at age twenty-three, Rank published *The Artist*, the first psychoanalytic book not written by Freud. A year earlier, Freud had hired the precocious Rank to be his secretary, virtually adopting him as a foster son, and paying his way for a PhD in Literature at the University of Vienna.

Grateful for Freud's generosity, Rank responded by publishing a stream of articles and books, advancing psychoanalytic thinking into almost every area of the arts and humanities. Freud would point to Rank's mastery of myth, symbols, art, philosophy, and world literature to show his critics that the validity of psychoanalysis did not hinge on Freud's autobiographical *The Interpretation of Dreams*, which, Freud knew, could not be accepted as scientific evidence (Marinelli & Mayer, 2003).

"His independence of me is greater than it appears," Freud told Jung in 1907; "very young, he has a good head and is thoroughly honest and open" (Lieberman, 1985, p. 98).

Freud was so impressed by Rank's erudition that in 1914 he invited his protégé to contribute two chapters, on poetry and myth, to the second edition of *The Interpretation of Dreams*; thereafter, Rank's name would appear under Freud's on the title page of the foundational text of psychoanalysis for the next fifteen years.

In 1914, Rank also published *The Double*, an existential study of identity, guilt, narcissism, the fear of death, the soul, and the desire for immortality. Dreams and movies speak a similar language, proposed Rank, who analysed H. H. Ewer's silent film *The Student of Prague*. "It may perhaps turn out," he wrote, becoming the first psychoanalytic movie critic, "that cinematography, which, in numerous ways reminds us of the dream-work, can also express certain psychological facts, which the writer is unable to describe with verbal clarity" (Rank, 1914, p. 4). The immortal soul, according to Rank, was the first "double" of the body. The "double" is a defence against the anxiety of death (*Todesangst*), an idea Rank would expand fifteen years later in *Will Therapy* (1929–1931) into "*Lebensangst*" and "*Todesangst*" (life fear and death fear).

After the Great War, Rank was the second most powerful man in the psychoanalytic movement. Vice-President of the Vienna Psychoanalytic Society, chief editor of the two leading psychoanalytic journals, *Zeitschrift* and *Imago*, director of Freud's publishing house, the Verlag, and senior training analyst in Vienna after Freud, Otto Rank was officially named by Freud to be his heir-apparent in the early 1920s.

"He is doing all the work," Freud reported to Ernest Jones in 1919, "performing the possible and impossible alike, I dare say, you know him for what he is, the truest, most reliable, most charming of helpers, the column, which is bearing the edifice" (Paskauskas, 1993, p. 353).

Jones, jealous of Rank's closeness to Freud, and terrified of Rank's power to shut down the English-language journals and publications that he spearheaded, took vengeance on Rank in his biography of Freud, published in the late 1950s. Asserting that Rank was never personally close to Freud, and that Rank was "psychotic," he brazenly lied about Rank, who had died in 1939 and could not defend himself (Lieberman & Kramer, 2012). Jones did not label Jung "psychotic," for fear that Jung, then still living, would sue him for libel.

Freud always marvelled at Rank's analytical skills and encouraged him, early on, to become the first lay analyst. At age twenty-six, Rank published "A dream that interprets itself" (1910), an interpretation so penetrating that Freud could not praise it too highly. "Perhaps the best example of the interpretation of a dream," rejoiced Freud in his *Introductory Lectures on Psycho-Analysis*, "is the one reported by Otto Rank consisting of two interrelated dreams dreamt by a young girl, which occupy about two pages of print: but their analysis extends to seventy-six pages. So I should need something like a whole term to conduct you through [it]" (1916–1917, p. 185).

This is the first English translation of Rank's masterpiece of dream interpretation, originally published in 1910 as "Ein Traum, der sich selbst deutet," in *Jahrbuch für psychoanalytische und psychopathologische Forschungen, 2* (2): 465–540.

After moving to Paris in 1926, in the wake of Freud's refusal to accept the preoedipal thesis of *The Trauma of Birth*, Rank travelled often to America to see patients and lecture at universities such as Harvard, Yale, the University of Minnesota, Stanford, and the University of Pennsylvania School of Social Work, where he taught relationship therapy as a professor from 1926 until his death in 1939.

In recent years, there's been a renaissance of interest in Otto Rank. Brutally attacked by orthodox Freudians like Ernest Jones and Peter Gay for his "anti-oedipal" views, Rank, according to more than one estimate, "will probably turn out to be the best mind that psychoanalysis contributed to intellectual history" (J. Jones, 1960, p. 219).

The Rankian revival began in 1973 with Ernest Becker's Pulitzer-Prize-winning *The Denial of Death*, a merger of Rank's post-Freudian writings on "life fear" and "death fear" with the existential thinking of Kierkegaard. "The idea of death, the fear of it, haunts the human animal like nothing else," said Becker (1973), "it is a mainspring of human activity—activity designed largely to avoid the fatality of death, to overcome it by denying in some way that it is the final destiny for man" (p. xvii).

"This is the terror," wrote Becker, summarising his thesis in one heart-stopping sentence, "to have emerged from nothing, to have a name, consciousness of self, deep inner feelings, an excruciating yearning for life and self-expression—and with all this yet to die" (ibid., p. 87). We are born to die. Only the expression of our creativity, argued Becker, drawing on Rank's writings in *Truth and Reality* (1929), *Will Therapy* (1929–1931), *Psychology and the Soul* (1930), *Modern Education* (1932b), *Art and Artist* (1932a), and *Beyond Psychology* (1941), allows us to transcend death—through the construction of time-defying monuments of art and culture, whose symbols provide meaning in a terrifying universe, helping us deny death and glimpse, if only faintly, the eternal.

"There's no substitute for reading Rank," said Becker (1973), "he is a mine for years of insights and pondering" (p. xii). On the dedication page of *Escape from Evil*, the companion volume to *The Denial of Death*, Becker (1975) wrote: "In memory of Otto Rank, whose thought may well prove to be the rarest gift of Freud's disciples to the world."

In 1982, Esther Menaker published the first comprehensive treatment of Rank's ideas. Rank, she concluded, was the unacknowledged forerunner of intersubjective, relationship, person-centred, existential, and short-term psychotherapies (Menaker, 1982).

In 1985, E. James Lieberman wrote the first full-scale biography of Rank, based on dozens of interviews with those who knew Rank. Following the pioneering research of Paul Roazen (1974), Lieberman uncovered a host of lies in Ernest Jones's treatment of Rank in his Freud biography. "The truth about Rank himself can scarcely be found in print," said Lieberman (1985), who was amazed at the abundance of errors concerning Rank's life and work in the literature of psychoanalysis (p. xv).

After the publication of the landmark studies of Otto Rank by Ernest Becker, Esther Menaker, and E. James Lieberman, previously forgotten or dismissed works by Rank were gradually rediscovered. New readings of Rank now appear regularly, as his therapeutic, cultural, existential, feminist, and spiritual writings are becoming more widely appreciated. For example:

- In 1990, Madelon Sprengnether's *The Spectral Mother: Freud, Feminism, and Psychoanalysis*, showed how Freud's refusal to see the preoedipal mother, as illuminated in Rank's *The Trauma of Birth*, "nearly effaces her"—and all other women—"from the drama of human development" (p. 3).
- In 1995, Matthew Fox, a post-denominational theologian with a large following worldwide, published "Otto Rank on the artistic journey as a spiritual journey, the spiritual journey as an artistic journey," making a case for Rank as "one of the great spiritual giants of the twentieth century ... He died a feminist and deeply committed to social justice in 1939. His work, more than any other psychologist's, provides the appropriate basis for Creation Spirituality" (Fox, 1995, p. 199).

- In 1996, Esther Menaker published *Separation, Will and Creativity: The Wisdom of Otto Rank*, the capstone of her decades of studying Rank and applying his thinking to intersubjective psychoanalysis, empathic relationships, spirituality, and women's issues.
- In 1996, Princeton University Press published my edited collection of Rank's American lectures, entitled *A Psychology of Difference*, a series of twenty-two talks delivered by Rank from 1924 to 1937 at universities such as Yale, Stanford, the University of Minnesota, and the University of Pennsylvania School of Social Work.
- In *A Meeting of Minds: Mutuality in Psychoanalysis*, Lewis Aron (1996) concluded that, along with Ferenczi, Rank "anticipated many of the distinguishing marks of contemporary relational theories" (p. 183).
- Over the span of a dozen years, Johns Hopkins University Press published English translations by E. James Lieberman and Gregory C. Richter of Rank's *Incest Theme in Literature and Legend* (in 1992 [1912]); *Psychology and the Soul* (in 1998 [1930]); and the second edition, previously untranslated, of Rank's *The Myth of the Birth of the Hero* (in 2004 [1922]).
- In 1998, Marina Leitner published a book-length study in German entitled *Freud, Rank und die Folgen* ("Freud, Rank and the consequences"), showing why the conflict between Freud and Rank over *The Trauma of Birth* was a pivotal event in the history of psychoanalysis.
- In 1998, Ludwig Janus edited a special issue of the German psychoanalytic journal *psychosozial* devoted to rediscovering the value of Otto Rank's ideas for psychoanalysis. Along with numerous publications on Rank's innovations as a therapist, Janus has been at the forefront of promoting prenatal and perinatal psychology for medicine, just as Peter Sloterdijk (1998), the most famous living philosopher in Germany after Jürgen Habermas, has made us aware of the cultural and symbolic "micro-sphere" of the womb.
- In *Reading Psychoanalysis: Freud, Rank, Ferenczi, Groddeck*, Peter Rudnytsky (2002) confirmed that Rank was the first object-relations theorist and therapist, a conclusion he had already reached a decade earlier (Rudnytsky, 1991) in *The Psychoanalytic Vocation: Rank, Winnicott, and the Legacy of Freud*.
- In 2002, Matthew Fox published *Creativity: Where the Divine and Human Meet*, which drew on Rank's *Art and Artist* to explore how

the expression of our creative will can promote ecumenism, ecologi-
cal, and social justice, and a rebirth of the cosmological wisdom of
the ancients. "To allow creativity its appropriate place in our lives
and our culture, our education and our family relationships," said
Fox (2002), "is to allow healing to happen at a profound level" (p. 9).

- In 2006, the French psychoanalytic journal *Le Coq-Héron*, under
the editorship of Judith Dupont, literary heir of Sándor Ferenczi,
published a special issue with the title, "Otto Rank, l'accoucheur du
sujet" ("Otto Rank, midwife of the subject").

- In 2008, Cnaan, Dichter, and Draine published the first history
of the University of Pennsylvania School of Social Work, showing
Rank's lasting influence on the leading American school of social
work. Penn's ideas on relationship therapy have been accepted by all
schools of social work worldwide.

- In 2008, the philosopher Maxine Sheets-Johnstone published *The
Roots of Morality*, which explored Rank's argument that "immortality ideologies" are our abiding response to the painful riddle of death.
For Rank, as for Ernest Becker, history is a succession of immortality ideologies, beginning with belief in the soul. Sheets-Johnstone
compared Rank's writings on the universality of soul-belief, introduced first in *The Double* and expanded later in *Psychology and the
Soul*, with the thinking of three major Western philosophers—René
Descartes, Martin Heidegger, and Jacques Derrida.

- In a 2010 study of Rank's *Will Therapy*, Dan Merkur observed in
Contemporary Psychoanalytic Studies, Volume 11, that "the rehabili-
tation of Rank's reputation and technical innovations within psychoanalysis awaited the rise in the 1980s of the American school of
relational psychoanalysis" (p. 53).

- In 2012, Johns Hopkins University Press published *The Letters of
Sigmund Freud and Otto Rank: Inside Psychoanalysis*, edited by me
and E. James Lieberman, correcting fabrications by Ernest Jones,
Rank's bitter rival for leadership of the psychoanalytic movement in
the early 1920s, in Jones's Freud biography.

- In 2012, Francisco Obaid published a comprehensive account in *The
International Journal of Psychoanalysis* (which had dismissed Rank's
ideas for almost a century) of the debate between Freud and Rank
over the relationship between anxiety and birth.

- In 2012, under the guest editorship of Judith Dupont, a special issue of *The American Journal of Psychoanalysis*, entitled "Recognizing Otto Rank, an innovator," was devoted to Rank's life and work.
- In 2013, in *The Psychoanalytic Review*, Rosemary Balsam showed that Rank, as an early feminist, was the first male analyst to see "childbirth as a central bodily female experience" (p. 713).
- In 2015, in *Psychoanalyse im Widerspruch*, I published the first comprehensive account of why Freud banished Rank.
- In 2016, in *The Psychoanalytic Review*, Daniel Sullivan published the first study of Rank's psychology of emotions.
- In 2017, Mark Griffiths published *The Challenge of Existential Social Work*, which highlighted Rank's lasting legacy for social work worldwide, beginning with the relationship therapy introduced in the late 1920s by Rank and Jessie Taft at the University of Pennsylvania School of Social Work.
- In 2017, in *Psychoanalyse im Widerspruch*, Ludwig Janus published Phoebe Crosby's account of her analysis with Rank in 1927.
- In 2018, Susan Lanzoni published *Empathy: A History*, showing how Ferenczi and Rank's advocacy of empathic understanding (*Einfühlung*) helped shape the client-centred practices of Taft and Carl Rogers.
- In 2023, in *The Humanistic Psychologist*, I published the first comprehensive account of Rank's influence on Rollo May (1958), the founder of existential therapy in America. An American mid-Westerner, Rollo May, I wrote, "brought a darkly tragic Rankian awareness of the existential unconscious into the conformist, anti-intellectual consciousness of America."
- In 2024, with Oxford University Press, I will publish *Otto Rank and the Creation of Modern Psychotherapy*, arguing that Rank, through his impact on Carl Rogers, Rollo May, and Irvin Yalom, is the creator of twenty-first-century psychotherapy. "I became infected with Rankian ideas," said Rogers, the most influential American psychotherapist of the twentieth century. "I have long considered Otto Rank to be *the* great unacknowledged genius in Freud's circle," said Rollo May, a leading American psychotherapist and public intellectual during the second half of the twentieth century. "I gasped at his prescience, when reading his works," said Irvin Yalom, the world's most famous existential psychotherapist, "especially his books,

Will Therapy and *Truth and Reality*." If the twentieth century was the century of Freud, then the twenty-first is shaping up to be the century of Rank.

- Over the last two decades, Hans-Jürgen Wirth, founder of Psychosozial-Verlag, has published five German-language works by Rank: *Kunst und Künstler* (in 2000 [1932a]), which originally appeared only in English (as *Art and Artist* in 1932); three volumes of *Technik der Psychoanalyse* (in 2006), the last two of which were published in English as *Will Therapy* in 1936; and *Das Trauma der Geburt* (in 2007). Wirth's German edition of the Freud–Rank letters was published in 2014, and a French translation, under the direction of Judith Dupont, appeared shortly thereafter. Other translations are now in preparation.

References

Aron, L. (1996). *A Meeting of Minds: Mutuality in Psychoanalysis.* Hillsdale: The Analytic Press.

Balsam, R. H. (2013). Freud, females, childbirth and dissidence: Margarite Hilferding, Karen Horney and Otto Rank. *The Psychoanalytic Review, 100*: 695–716.

Balsam, R. H. (2016). The war on women in psychoanalytic theory: Past to present. In: C. Lamont, R. A. King, S. Abrams, P. M. Brinich, & R. Knight (Eds.), *The War Against Women in Psychoanalytic Culture.* New Haven: Yale University Press, pp. 83–107.

Becker, E. (1973). *The Denial of Death*, with a foreword by Sam Keen. New York: The Free Press (1997 paperback edition).

Becker. E. (1975). *Escape from Evil.* New York: The Free Press.

Cnaan, R. A., Dichter, M. E., & Draine, J. (2008). *A Century of Social Work and Social Welfare at Penn.* Philadelphia: University of Pennsylvania Press.

Crosby, P., & Janus, L. (2017). Eine Analyse bei Otto Rank. *Forum der Psychoanalyse: Zeitschrift für psychodynamische Theorie und Praxis, 33*: 447–457.

Dupont, J. (Ed.) (2006). Otto Rank, l'accoucheur du sujet. *Le Coq-Héron, 187*: 1–79.

Dupont, J. (Ed.) (2012). Recognizing Otto Rank, an innovator. *The American Journal of Psychoanalysis, 72*: 315–417.

Fox, M. (1995). Otto Rank on the artistic journey as a spiritual journey, the spiritual journey as an artistic journey. In: M. Fox, *Wrestling with the Prophets: Essays on Creation Spirituality and Everyday Life*. San Francisco: Harper Collins, pp. 199–242.

Fox, M. (2002). *Creativity: Where the Divine and the Human Meet*. New York: Jeremy Tarcher/Putnam.

Freud, S. (1916–1917). *Introductory Lectures on Psycho-Analysis*. In: *The Standard Edition of the Complete Psychological Works*. London: Hogarth.

Griffiths, M. (2017). *The Challenges of Existential Social Work*. New York: Red Globe Press.

Janus, L. (Ed.) (1998). Die Wiederentdeckung Otto Ranks für die Psychoanalyse. *Psychosozial, 73, 21*(III): 1–168.

Jones, J. (1960). Otto Rank: A forgotten heresy. *Commentary, 30*: 219–229.

Kramer, R. (2015). "I am boiling with rage": Why did Freud banish Rank? *Psychoanalyse im Widerspruch, 53*: 31–44.

Kramer, R. (2023). Discovering the existential unconscious: Rollo May encounters Otto Rank. *The Humanistic Psychologist, 51*(1): 15–35.

Kramer, R. (2024). *Otto Rank and the Creation of Modern Psychotherapy*. Oxford: Oxford University Press.

Lanzoni, S. (2018). *Empathy: A History*. New Haven: Yale University Press.

Leitner, M. (1998). *Freud, Rank und die Folgen: ein Schlüsselkonflikt für die Psychoanalyse*. Vienna: Turia + Kant.

Lieberman, E. J. (1985). *Acts of Will: The Life and Work of Otto Rank*. New York: The Free Press. See also: E. J. Lieberman, *Otto Rank: Leben und Werk*. Gießen: Psychosozial-Verlag, 2014 (2nd edn.).

Lieberman, E. J., & Kramer, R. (2012). *The Letters of Sigmund Freud and Otto Rank: Inside Psychoanalysis*. Trans. G. C. Richter. Baltimore: Johns Hopkins University Press. See also: *Sigmund Freud und Otto Rank: Ihre Beziehung im Spiegel des Briefwechsels 1906–1925*. Eds. E. J. Lieberman & R. Kramer. Gießen: Psychosozial-Verlag, 2014.

Marinelli, L., & Mayer. A. (2003). *Dreaming by the Book: Freud's* The Interpretation of Dreams *and the History of the Psychoanalytic Movement*. Trans. S. Fairfield. New York: Other Press.

Menaker, E. (1982). *Otto Rank: A Rediscovered Legacy*. New York: Columbia University Press.

Menaker, E. (1996). *Separation, Will and Creativity: The Wisdom of Otto Rank*. New York: Jason Aronson.

Merkur, D. (2010). Otto Rank's *Will Therapy*. In: D. Merkur (Ed.), *Contemporary Psychoanalytic Studies: Explorations of the Psychoanalytic Mystics* (Vol. 11, pp. 53–70). Amsterdam and New York: Rodopi.

Obaid, F. P. (2012). Sigmund Freud and Otto Rank: Debates and confrontations about anxiety and birth. *International Journal of Psychoanalysis, 93*: 449–471.

Paskauskas, R. A. (Ed.) (1993). *The Complete Correspondence of Sigmund Freud and Ernest Jones, 1908–1939.* Cambridge, MA: Harvard University Press.

Rank, O. (1910). "Ein Traum, der sich selbst deutet," *Jahrbuch für Psychoanalytische und Psychopathologische Forschungen,* 2 (2): 465–540.

Rank, O. (1912). *The Incest Theme in Literature and Legend: Fundamentals of a Psychology of Literary Creation.* Trans. G. C. Richter. Baltimore: Johns Hopkins University Press, 1992.

Rank, O. (1914). *The Double: A Psychoanalytic Study.* Trans. H. Tucker. London: Maresfield Library, 1989.

Rank, O. (1922). *The Myth of the Birth of the Hero: A Psychological Exploration of Myth.* Expanded and updated edition. Trans. G. C. Richter & E. J. Lieberman. Baltimore: Johns Hopkins University Press, 2004.

Rank, O. (1924). *The Trauma of Birth.* New York: Dover, 1993. See also: O. Rank, *Das Trauma der Geburt und seine Bedeutung für die Psychoanalyse.* Gießen: Psychosozial-Verlag, 2007.

Rank, O. (1926–1931). *Technik der Psychoanalyse, I–III.* Eds. L. Janus & H.-J. Wirth. Gießen: Psychosozial-Verlag, 2006.

Rank, O. (1927–1928). *Genetische Psychologie, Vols. I–II.* Leipzig and Vienna: Deuticke.

Rank, O. (1929). *Truth and Reality.* New York: W. W. Norton, 1978.

Rank, O. (1930). *Psychology and the Soul: A Study of the Origin, Conceptual Evolution and Nature of the Soul.* Trans. G. C. Richter & E. J. Lieberman. Baltimore: Johns Hopkins University Press, 1998.

Rank, O. (1932a). *Art and Artist: Creative Urge and Personality Development.* Trans. C. Atkinson. New York: Alfred A. Knopf. See also: O. Rank, *Kunst und Künstler: Studien zur Genese und Entwicklung des Schaffensdranges.* Ed. H. Wirth. Gießen: Psychosozial-Verlag, 2000.

Rank, O. (1932b). *Modern Education.* Trans. M. Moxon. New York: Alfred A. Knopf.

Rank, O. (1936). *Will Therapy: An Analysis of the Therapeutic Process in Terms of Relationship.* Trans. J. Taft. New York: W. W. Norton, 1978. [Translation of *Technik der Psychoanalyse, II: Die analytische Reaktion in ihren kon-struktiven Elementen*. Leipzig and Vienna: Deuticke, 1929; and *Technik der Psychoanalyse, III: Die Analyse des Analytikers und seiner Rolle in der Gesamtsituation*. Leipzig and Vienna: Deuticke, 1931.

Rank, O. (1941). *Beyond Psychology*. New York: Dover, 1958.

Rank, O. (1996). *A Psychology of Difference: The American Lectures*. Ed. R. Kramer, with a foreword by Rollo May. Princeton: Princeton University Press.

Roazen, P. (1974). *Freud and His Followers*. New York: Alfred A. Knopf.

Rudnytsky, P. L. (1991). *The Psychoanalytic Vocation: Rank, Winnicott, and the Legacy of Freud*. New Haven: Yale University Press.

Rudnytsky, P. L. (2002). *Reading Psychoanalysis: Freud, Rank, Ferenczi, Groddeck*. Ithaca: Cornell University Press.

Sheets-Johnstone, M. (2008). *The Roots of Morality*. University Park: Pennsylvania State University Press.

Sloterdijk, P. (1998). *Sphären I: Blasen. Mikrosphärologie*. Frankfurt am Main: Suhrkamp Verlag. See also: P. Sloterdijk (2011). *Bubbles: Spheres, Vol. I: Microspherology*. Los Angeles: Semiotext(e).

Sprengnether, M. (1990). *The Spectral Mother: Freud, Feminism, and Psycho-analysis*. Ithaca: Cornell University Press.

Sullivan, D. (2016). Person–environment mergence and separation: Otto Rank's psychology of emotion. *Psychoanalytic Review, 103*: 743–770.

Chronology of Otto Rank's life (1884–1939) and work

Robert Kramer

1884	Born in Vienna, 22 April.
1905	Sends Freud a manuscript entitled *The Artist*, using the word *artist* in as comprehensive a sense as Freud had used the word *sexuality*.
1906	Accepts Freud's offer to be secretary of the fledgling Vienna Psychoanalytical Society, the first paid position in the movement; is virtually adopted by Freud as a "foster son"; and is asked by Freud to devote himself to the non-medical side of psychoanalysis, becoming the first lay analyst in the world.
1907	Publishes *The Artist*, the first psychoanalytic work not written by Freud.
1909	Publishes *The Myth of the Birth of the Hero*, with a section on the "family romance" contributed by Freud.
1911	Helps Freud edit and revise the third edition of *The Interpretation of Dreams*.
1911	Publishes *The Lohengrin Saga*, for which he later receives a PhD from the University of Vienna, the first dissertation ever published on a psychoanalytic theme.

1912   Publishes *The Incest Theme in Literature and Legend: Fundamentals of a Psychology of Literary Creation*, a 685-page study of the Oedipus complex throughout world literature.

1912   Becomes the youngest ring holder of the Secret Committee—Abraham, Ferenczi, Sachs, Jones (and later, Eitingon)—formed by Freud as a Politburo to defend the cause against "heretics" like Adler and Jung.

1912   Co-founds and serves as the main editor of *Imago* and *Internationale Zeitschrift für Psychoanalyse*, the two leading journals of the cause.

1913   Publishes, with Sachs, *The Significance of Psychoanalysis for the Mental Sciences*.

1914   Contributes two chapters, on literature and myth, to the fourth edition of *The Interpretation of Dreams*, his name now appearing (until 1929) below Freud's on the title page.

1914   Publishes *The Double*, an existential study of identity, guilt, narcissism, the fear of death, the soul, and the desire for immortality.

1916–1918   Serves as editor-in-chief of *Krakauer Zeitung*, the official army newspaper in Poland.

1918   Marries Tola Minzer, twenty-three, in Poland.

1919   Returns to Vienna to edit *Imago* and *Internationale Zeitschrift* and is asked by Freud to become director of Verlag, the newly created international psychoanalytic publishing house, and Vice-President of the Vienna Psychoanalytical Society.

1919   Begins full-time practice as a lay analyst and conducts training analyses for visiting American psychiatrists.

1919   Helene, his only child, is born.

1922   Is designated by Freud to be his heir.

1922–1923   Drafts with Ferenczi, now his best friend, *The Development of Psychoanalysis*, which advocates the curative effect of the "here-and-now" emotional experience (*Erlebnis*) between analyst and patient over intellectual understanding (*Einsicht*) of the infantile past via interpretations offered by a neutral analyst.

1923   Is informed, immediately after diagnosis, of Freud's life-threatening cancer of the jaw.

1924   Publishes, with Ferenczi, *The Development of Psychoanalysis*, criticising the "fanaticism for interpreting" among analysts: "the actual analytic task," they say, "was neglected."

1924   Publishes *The Trauma of Birth*, coining the term "preoedipal" and claiming that the "ambivalent" preoedipal relationship between mother and child is the heart of transference, thereby relegating fear and love of the oedipal father to a secondary place.

1924   Sails for the United States in April and lectures on his preoedipal theory before the American Psychoanalytic Association and other audiences.

1924   From the United States, in an August letter, denies Freud's charge that he has "excluded the father; naturally that is not the case and absolutely cannot be, it would be nonsense. I have only attempted to give him the correct place."

1925   Confesses in January to an oedipal neurosis, "occasioned by the dangerous illness of the Professor," after a soul-baring *Erlebnis* therapy in December 1924 with Freud, who forgives him.

1925   At a seminar for the New York Psychoanalytic Society, insists, "The only real new viewpoint in [my] contribution [is] the concept of the pre-Oedipus level."

1926   Recants his oedipal neurosis, resigns from his editorial and administrative positions, and moves to Paris in April to start a new practice, severing all ties with medical psychoanalysis and the Secret Committee.

1926   Delivers a series of lectures before the New York School of Social Work, based on Volume 1 of his forthcoming work, *Genetische Psychologie* (1927), whose opening sentence reads: "This book is a direct continuation ... of my new vision in psychoanalytic theory and therapy."

1926   In his New York lectures, accuses Freud of repressing the role of the powerful will of the preoedipal mother: "The 'bad mother' he has never seen, but only the later displacement of her to the father, who therefore plays such an

	omnipotent part in his theory … The 'strict mother' thus forms the real nucleus of the super-ego."
1927	Delivers a series of lectures before the University of Pennsylvania School of Social Work, based on Volume 2 of his forthcoming work, *Genetische Psychologie* (1928).
1927	In a lecture at the University of Pennsylvania, announces that he is no longer "going back" to the preoedipal mother: many neurotics belong to the "creative type" but "have failed in the formation and development of their own personality"; they are, in essence, failed artists.
1927	In other University of Pennsylvania lectures, defines love in terms of the I–Thou relationship: "The love of the Thou … places a value on one's own I. Love abolishes egoism, it merges the self in the other to find it again enriched in one's own I … One can really only love the one who accepts our own self as it is, indeed will not have it otherwise than it is, and whose self we accept as it is."
	In the same lecture, defines guilt as a "special emotion," lying on "the boundary line … between the severing and uniting feelings; [therefore,] it is also the most important representative of the relation between inner and outer, I and Thou, the Self and the World."
1929–1931	Delivers another series of lectures at the University of Pennsylvania based on two books published in English as *Will Therapy* and *Truth and Reality*, claiming that "the real I, or self with its own power, the will, is left out" of psychoanalysis, but stressing repeatedly that "will and guilt are the two complementary sides of one and the same phenomenon"— which he calls the will–guilt problem.
1929–1931	Reframing Freud's "economic" metaphor of drive, asserts in *Will Therapy* that the neurotic (or *artiste manqué*) "bribes" life itself—for which we all have to "pay" with death: because of extreme guilt and anxiety, the neurotic hurls a "Big No" at the consciousness of living, refusing the loan, life, in order to escape payment of the debt, death.
1930	Publishes *Seelenglaube und Psychologie*, drawing on Bohr's "theory of complementarity" and Heisenberg's

"uncertainty principle" to demonstrate that quantum physics has proved that the human being "simply lies beyond lawfulness, and cannot be fully comprehended or explained by the causality either of natural or social science"—or "the cause" of psychoanalysis.

1930   In a Washington, DC lecture, attended by a large international audience, says that while he has stopped calling himself a psychoanalyst, "I am no longer trying to prove that Freud was wrong and I am right ... It is not a question of whose interpretation is correct—because there is no such thing as *the* interpretation or only *one* psychological truth."

1930   Is removed by the American Psychoanalytic Association from its list of honorary members, immediately after the Washington, DC lecture, on a motion by President A. A. Brill, seconded by Vice-President Harry Stack Sullivan: re-analysis of his analysands by Freudians is required for them to retain membership in the American Psychoanalytic Association.

1932   Publishes *Art and Artist*, showing that only the "human creative impulse" can constructively harmonise "the fundamental dualism" of life and death, a dualism Rank explores along many lines: the wish for—and fear of—separation, the wish for—and fear of—union, the oscillation between life *Angst* and death *Angst*, independence and dependence, I and Thou, and, most importantly, the "will–guilt problem."

1932   Publishes *Modern Education*, concluding that "psychoanalysis is as conservative as it appeared revolutionary; for its founder is a rebellious son who defends paternal authority, a revolutionary who, from fear of his own rebellious son-ego, took refuge in the security of the father role."

1935   Moves from Paris, where he analyses Anaïs Nin, Henry Miller, and many other writers and artists, to New York and continues practising psychotherapy and lecturing in the United States.

1936   Meets a young Carl Rogers during a three-day workshop in Rochester, NY, and influences him to abandon Freudian technique for "client-centred" and "relationship" therapy. Shortly thereafter, Rogers becomes the first humanistic psychotherapist in the US. "I became infected with Rankian ideas," Rogers says.

1936   Through his analyst Harry Bone (who trained with Rank in Paris), Rollo May studies Rank's writings on love and will and, shortly thereafter, becomes the first existential psychotherapist in the US. "I have long considered Otto Rank to be *the* great unacknowledged genius in Freud's circle," attests May in his foreword to *A Psychology of Difference* (published in 1996), a collection of twenty-two lectures that Rank delivered from 1924 to 1938 at universities throughout America, including Yale, Stanford, the University of Minnesota, and the University of Pennsylvania School of Social Work.

1937–1939   Drafts *Beyond Psychology* (published posthumously in 1941), advocating a "psychology of difference" as opposed to Freud's "psychology of likeness."

1939   Divorces Tola Rank and marries Estelle Buel, his secretary, in July.

1939   Dies in New York from a reaction to an injection of a sulfa (antibacterial) drug, on 31 October—one month after Freud's death in London, from an injection of morphine by his personal physician, on 23 September, the Jewish Day of Atonement.

1941   *Beyond Psychology* is published posthumously by friends of Rank.

1992   Gregory C. Richter translates and publishes Rank's 1912 edition of *The Incest Theme in Literature and Legend: Fundamentals of a Psychology of Literary Creation.*

1996   Robert Kramer writes a forty-three-page introduction to Rank's *A Psychology of Difference: The American Lectures.*

1998   E. J. Lieberman and Gregory C. Richter translate and publish Rank's 1930 book *Seelenglaube und Psychologie* under the title *Psychology and the Soul: A Study of the Origin, Conceptual Evolution, and Nature of the Soul.*

2012   E. J. Lieberman and Robert Kramer edit and publish *The Letters of Sigmund Freud and Otto Rank: Inside Psycho-analysis*, translated by Gregory C. Richter.

2024   Robert Kramer edits, introduces, and publishes Rank's "Ein Traum, der sich selbst deutet," translated by Gregory C. Richter.

A DREAM THAT INTERPRETS ITSELF

Otto Rank

Truly the fabric of mental fleece
Resembles a weaver's masterpiece,
Where a thousand threads one treadle throws,
Where fly the shuttles hither and thither.
Unseen the threads are knit together.
And an infinite combination grows.
(Goethe, Faust, lines 1922–1927)

The technique of psychoanalysis

A young woman of my acquaintance, not a neurotic, who had heard of my interest in the problem of dreams, related to me a "poetical dream, as beautiful as a fairy tale," and half-jokingly asked me to test on it my skills of interpretation.

When dream analyses are undertaken in this way, without any therapeutic purpose (in the case of neurotics) or with a purely theoretical purpose (in the case of one's own dreams), the conditions are usually so unfavourable that the results almost never have sufficient evidential value or meaning for scientific use.

In this case, too, in requesting an interpretation of her dream, the dreamer had no practical theoretical interest and no theoretical scientific interest.

Rather, beyond admiration of the really beautiful dream imagery, she expected my admission that it was uninterpretable; at most, she expected an interpretation along the lines of ordinary popular superstition, telling her of her future good fortune.

As for myself, when confronted with this attractive but rather purposeless task, I felt no desire to increase by one the number of impeccable dream analyses appearing in the psychoanalytic literature by presenting an analysis characterised mainly by its defects and incompleteness.

Despite these limitations, the following dream analysis proved worthy of publication here: due to an unusual and remarkable circumstance, it is to be preferred over similar amateur attempts.

The dream that provides the topic for this article has, in fact, the special characteristic of allowing its real meaning to show through almost undisguised, providing us quite openly with a portion of the interpretation that would otherwise require laborious psychoanalytic work.

In order to show the special sense in which this is meant, and how far such a view is theoretically justified, we will need to go more deeply into some of the essential points in the technique of dream analysis established by Freud.

As is well known, besides the remembered "manifest dream content," Freud distinguishes the "latent dream thoughts," which are identified through analytic work. It is only through the latent dream thoughts that the dream characteristics of the manifest dream content, violently disputed as they are, and especially the most important one, wish fulfilment, have validity.

It is then appropriate and fully in accord with psychological circumstances to divide the "latent" dream content into two groups: the unconscious proper, overlaid by other mental material, and thus deeply hidden from the dreamer; and second, the other group of dream thoughts, more easily accessible to the conscious faculties, which we may think of as located in that mental region described in dream theory as the preconscious (Freud, 1909a, p. 334).

Within limits, these two sources of material, not sharply distinguished in practice, can be separated without difficulty during the analysis. At the beginning of a dream analysis, it is easy for dreamers, by concentrating their attention, to recall quickly and without perceptible resistance a number of ideas which, to their great surprise, had escaped their conscious thought, but which, nevertheless, stand in close connection with the dream content and give it meaning.

Given further unhindered thought, from these ideas connected with the manifest dream elements, a close chain of association leads to the ultimate dream-forming elements hidden deeply in the unconscious; soon, one will note from the sparsity and hesitancy of the ideas, and from the strong resistance to their coming into consciousness, how close one is getting to the more deeply hidden emotions (preconscious or entirely unconscious).

Soon, the flow of ideas ceases completely, dreamers are no longer able to bring new material into the realm of consciousness, and the work of interpretation is apparently ended. But Freud has emphatically warned against being satisfied with such premature solutions, even "if one has in one's hands a complete dream interpretation that is full of meaning and coherent, and provides information about all the elements of the dream content" (Freud, 1909a, p. 322).

Indeed, a complete interpretation of dreams requires exposing at least one infantile wish (drive) originating in the deepest region of the unconscious, which in infancy was an actual wish, later repressed into the unconscious, and which now seeks to realise itself again, though in distorted form, in dream life.

The more one deals with the explanation of dreams, the sooner one must acknowledge that most of the dreams of adults deal with sexual material and bring erotic wishes to expression. "But the theory of the psychoneuroses asserts with absolute certainty that these can only be infantile sexual wishes that are repressed in the developmental stages of childhood, and which are then capable of renewal in later developmental stages … and which thus supply the driving forces for the development of all psychoneurotic symptoms" (Freud, 1909a, p. 376).

In the first edition of *The Interpretation of Dreams* (1900), Freud "left the question unanswered whether the demands of the sexual and of the infantile can be relevant for the theory of dreams," but later insight, deepened by increased experience, has made this undeniable. In a remarkable addition in the second edition (1909a, p. 197), Freud discusses this as follows: "The more one occupies oneself with the solution of dreams, the sooner one must recognise that most of the dreams of adults deal with sexual material and express erotic wishes … Only those who really analyse dreams—i.e. by moving forward from the manifest content into the latent dream thoughts—can truly judge this matter."

"Let us say at the outset that this fact is no surprise, but is in full agreement with our principles of dream interpretation. Beginning in childhood, no other drive has had to undergo as much repression as the sexual drive with its numerous components; from no other drive arise so many and such strong unconscious wishes, which in a state of sleep work to produce dreams" (Freud, 1910a).

Therefore, no one will be surprised that the work of interpretation is by no means always successful in discovering the actually unconscious-infantile sexual wish impulses, and that accordingly

> the question as to whether every dream can be interpreted is in practice to be answered in the negative. It must not be forgotten that in the work of interpretation one is opposed by mental forces that distort the dream. It becomes thus a question of proportionate strength, whether with intellectual interest, capacity for self-mastery, psychological knowledge, and experience in dream interpretation one can overcome these inner resistances. This is always possible to a certain extent—far enough at least to be convinced that the dream is a structure full of meaning—and generally far enough to gain some idea of this meaning.
>
> (Freud, 1909a, p. 322)

We are well justified in supposing that this will generally be possible when dealing with material originating in the preconscious—material which can be described, in contrast with the primitive sexual character of the unconscious, as cultural material.

Indeed, it includes not only the whole present personality of the individual, with all its interests and relationships, but also seems to reflect, as if by historical development, the whole superstructure of sublimation that cultural life builds over primitive drive life.

To illustrate the evasive dynamic conditions determining the degree of consciousness that a thought may attain, let us use the helpful image of sharply divided mental regions, neglecting the barely noticeable over-laps. Then it may be said that the manifest dream content arises from the conscious, the cultural dream elements from the preconscious, and the primitive sexual dream material from the unconscious.

The elements belonging to the different strata are, of course, of com-pletely unequal value, and should be formally separated in the presenta-tion of a complete dream analysis. Here, it should be noticed that dream thoughts arising from the preconscious, some of them also being cur-rent dream thoughts, display wish fulfilment as their most essential characteristic.

This fact is in complete accord with a fundamental principle of dream theory, which assumes, as the necessary condition for the shap-ing of dreams, the involvement of innocuous wish-fulfilment fantasies; these fantasies are usually self-serving, ambitious, or revengeful, or allay recent concerns. But we must note the important corollary that the dream would not arise if the preconscious wish could not use an analogous unconscious wish as a reinforcement.

Only seldom is it possible to analyse a dream so far that the over-lay of the separate wish fantasies, so unequal in value, becomes clear. (A fine example of this type is provided by the dream interpretation in Freud, 1905.) When there is no therapeutic need or special scientific goal, one will usually be content to uncover the preconscious material, which indeed is quite convincing and, as shown in Freud's *The Interpre-tation of Dreams*, completely suffices for the theoretical treatment of the problem of dreams.

However, psychoanalysis must always expose the ultimate roots of the dream, toward whose discovery dreamers themselves can con-tribute almost nothing: in fact, dreamers' inability to bring these into consciousness is one of the conditions for the formation of dreams. In certain cases, the difficulty of reaching the actual unconscious sources of the dream has led some psychoanalysts to seek ways to lighten or shorten this troublesome and tedious process, and it might seem that these attempts were not without prospect of success.

The development of psychoanalytic technique and a striking uni-formity in certain findings have made it possible to make highly secure conjectures about certain parts of the actually unconscious meaning of the dream.

These conjectures were made in the analyses of the dreams of neurotic persons, given a detailed knowledge of the lives and mental state of these patients, and also based on typical modes of activity of the unconscious mind and the mastery of a general symbolic language especially eloquent in dreams.

Such an attempt, dictated by the needs of the practitioner, has recently been undertaken by Stekel (1909). If his article was met with incomprehension on the part of readers not completely familiar with the language of the unconscious, this is because, in the chain of associations leading from the manifest dream content through the broad realm of preconscious thought to the unconscious roots, certain elements more easily accessible to general understanding were disregarded, and the primitive sexual meaning of the dream, a meaning usually distorted in the dream content by a strange symbolism, was directly exposed.

From the standpoint of the practitioner, it naturally seems justifiable, and sometimes even necessary, to disregard the "cultural layer" in certain dreams and, based on empirically established, general human symbolism, to translate individual elements of the manifest content out of the language of the unconscious.

This "cultural layer," with which the physician is usually familiar in any case from the psychoanalytic treatment of the patient, is essential for a theoretical appreciation of the dream and is highly instructive in considering the historical development of the layering of mental life.

For in actual practice, the tedious unwinding of the entire chain of thoughts serves only to direct the conscious thoughts of the patient, along the associatively established pathways, to the ultimate unconscious dream-forming complexes standing at the far end of this sequence.

And since the intermediate portion of the analytical work still does not deliver pure actual dream thoughts, but also the so-called *collateral thoughts*, "not all of which must necessarily have been involved in the formation of dreams" (Freud, 1909a, p. 226), one can, without substantial harm to the understanding of the dream, spare oneself time and trouble by using such an abbreviated procedure in certain cases. In using this method, though, one must be careful not to stray too far from a secure empirical foundation.

If, after these technical preliminaries, we turn again to the present dream, we may characterise in the following way the nature of its self-interpretation, the features that distinguish the dream, and their theoretical meaning. The self-interpretation of the dream will mainly be limited to exposing its primitive sexual roots—an exposure brought about in this case by the dream itself, independent of translation by the analyst.

It was just this part of the material that was successful in forging an open passage through the distorting veil of the dream; this is connected with the most prominent special feature of this dream, but thanks to another of its special features also casts a decisive light on the nature of dreams in general as related to sexual wish-fulfilment. The first of these special features is that the dream ends with an orgasm.

This characteristic, confining its evidential value to a small group of dreams, is, however, compensated by a second circumstance distinguishing this orgasmic dream from many other similar ones.

This dream consists of two parts separated in content as well as in time; they were both dreamt on the same night one after the other, and are closely connected in meaning, as regularly occurs in dreams, but only the second part can be called an orgasmic dream in a narrow sense.

It is this second part that, by virtue of the characteristic frankness of most orgasmic dreams, provides the correct interpretation of the first part—exactly that part of the meaning that is hardest to access through psychoanalysis because it is blocked by such deeply rooted mental forces as "shame, disgust, and aesthetic and moral groups of ideas" (Freud, 1910a, p. 38).

It would be possible to reach this core of the dream, though with difficulty, via self-analyses. As for other persons, this would only be possible with neurotics undergoing psychoanalytic treatment: in their case, the texture of the mind is, so to speak, thoroughly loosened, and given the intense desire to regain health is, in the long run, unable to resist the emergence of the unconscious into consciousness.

With a healthy person, whose normal feminine character is supported by precisely the mental reaction formations previously mentioned, it would seem quite impossible to bring these ultimate and completely buried elements of dream meaning to the light of day except when, as in this case, especially favourable circumstances characterise the attempt, which would otherwise be nearly hopeless.

It is due to these favourable conditions that our interpretive work need not proceed as usual from the isolated dream elements and the dreamer's ideas about them, which supply the original dream thoughts cut up and scattered in various contexts.

Rather, our interpretive work can start from the unconscious complexes shining through with unusual clarity and thus can, in each case, view the thematically connected material in the total context of its complexes. The ideas contributed by the dreamer, and drawn from recent events of daily life and the preconscious, serve only to complete and confirm the observed content of those complexes. [*The mode of presentation below attempts to convey the unique character of the dream and of the interpretive technique.*]

Our interest in this dream, distinguished by its so unusual features, is heightened by the theoretical value that must be ascribed to it. This theoretical value does not lie so much in the dream providing new data we could not have found in *The Interpretation of Dreams*. Rather, given its many peculiarities, it seems extremely well fitted to serve as a crucial test of the results that have already become known.

The clear presentation of its most secret meaning, a presentation occurring without the prejudicial intervention of the trained analyst, places us, with this dream, in the superior situation of being able to allow an interpretation of the dream to present itself to us uninfluenced in its most essential points by theoretical prejudices; thus, we are convinced of the extent to which the much-contested assertions and expectations of dream theory are correct.

It may be said in advance that this test proves favourable beyond expectation for the theory in question. It not only demonstrates, as it were, visually, the correctness of certain assumptions about the structure of the mental apparatus, while providing insight into the mental processes of dream formation, but also demonstrates the unassailability of the fundamental axioms of dream interpretation theory.

And this test can also persuade practitioners that they can, with amazing certitude, utilise the technical guidance and devices of Freud and his school for the interpretation of dream images which, at first, seem incomprehensible or even meaningless.

The dream and its interpretation

The dreamer relates the dream in the following words:

Part 1

I was in a royal palace as governess. The queen [*In later repetitions: "the lady"*], an older woman wearing a Chinese gown with a long train, was to go on a journey. I had to go away from the child to take leave of her. [*Later: "I don't know whether it was a boy or a girl."*]

To bid her farewell, I was supposed to lie down on the floor, but I wouldn't do so. Then she beat me on the face with a switch: only then did I lie right down, my nose touching the floor. I thought to myself: "What a fine post this has turned out to be!"

And now she beat me so it hurt. Then she extended her hand to me, and I kissed it. She then ordered a female attendant to take me, as a reward, into a lilac room [*Later: "a Chinese lilac room"*], a room otherwise forbidden.

As I entered, I was surprised that I wasn't being treated so badly after all: I had been granted the honour of examining this room. The attendant told me there were also birds here, and suddenly I saw a splendid bird flying toward me from behind. It settled down beside me; it had a long tail and strutted about proudly and gracefully like a wagtail [a slender songbird, typically living by water, with a long tail that it frequently wags up and down (Translator's Note)]. Its colour was lilac, like the room.

Then, I saw green trees like oleanders [poisonous evergreen shrubs (Translator's Note)], in blue pots before one entrance to the room, and the sun was shining. [*Later: "Through this doorlike opening I saw a garden and thought: 'God, if only I could go into that garden'—but I didn't go in."*]

Meanwhile, the tutor, a tall thin man, had also taken leave of the queen and was also allowed to examine the room. The queen told him he would have to wait until I came out, but he wanted to go in anyway, and the attendant said she would first have to lock the door. Then it was unlocked again and in he went.

The attendant (or chambermaid) was given 20 kreuzers as a reward. Then I was directed by the queen to a pink room, with a lovely pink wash basin. (The first reception room was yellow.)

I surprised the king, a dark handsome young man, while he was brushing his hair. [*Later: "I first saw him in the mirror, and then in person. He was brushing his hair up; it was still wet and standing on end."*] He said: "Pardon, this is not your room." I excused myself and went out, thinking: "The king is such a handsome man, and she is such an old woman. He's certainly not a good match for her."

Then I met him again in the reception room, and he turned around toward me as though he were in love with me. (I, too, could easily have fallen in love with him.) He said that he, too, was going away. [*Later: "In the yellow room, he once again looked in the mirror as if to convince himself that he was attractive to me."*]

I said in amazement: "So, you're going away?" "Yes," he said, "I'm going away." The chambermaid had to pack her master's things quickly. Whether they went away, I don't know. Afterwards, I didn't see the child again. There the dream ended.

On hearing this beautiful and intriguing dream, I would hardly suppose any clearly erotic wishes or bluntly sexual situations behind it, although it does not lack isolated allusions to the more delicate eroticism that might appear in a fairy tale, for example.

If, like me, one is somewhat familiar with the personal circumstances of the dreamer, it will not be hard to perceive the superficial wish-fulfilment tendency of the dream.

The dreamer has been away from her parents' home for several years, earns her own living, and is actually employed as a governess. At the time of the dream, she is unemployed and is very actively engaged in searching for a new position. Of course, she wants a "good position," with as distinguished a family as possible (royal palace), where there are plenty of servants (companion, tutor, chambermaid), where she has her own nicely furnished (pink) room and other advantages too (garden), where she is honoured (the honour of viewing the lilac room) and correspondingly well paid (20 kreuzers).

The dream shows her the most complete fulfilment of this wish fantasy: she is in a royal palace as governess. In her profession, one can rise no higher. In achieving her less ambitious real-world goals, however, reality presents her with more difficulties than she would like. She cannot even find a permanent and pleasing position in a better middle-class home, but is very soon in conflict with the lady of the house, and generally leaves her position due to advances by one of the male residents.

The dream does not fail to remind her of these drawbacks of her profession—how strictly one is treated by the lady (beating), how one must grovel before her (lying on the floor),[20] how one must act nicely toward her (kissing her hand) and sweetly toward the master (falling in love) if one wishes for a reward.

The emphasis on these disturbing trains of thought seems to contradict the tendency for wish-fulfilment, but was immediately resolved when I recognised that they only serve to help a second wish fantasy break through.

These trying circumstances and her worries about a secure future had recently made the dreamer wonder whether it would not be better to look for a husband instead of a position, and to establish a home of her own, naturally as distinguished and comfortable as possible, whose ideal image is to be found in the scenery of the dream.[6]

I would not expect to find the young woman's fantasies about the choice of a husband to have lower aspirations than her thoughts about a permanent position.

The man she wishes for herself must, of course, be young, handsome, and loving, and also as rich and distinguished as possible (a king).

In connection with previous daydreams of waking conscious life, the dream also shows her how to realise this fantasy typical of a young woman. The master of the house (the king), whose wife is much too old ("He's certainly not a good match for her"), falls in love with the young woman; nor would she be averse to giving him her love.

But here again disturbing factors enter the mix: the strict mistress of the house effectively blocks such an unwanted rivalry (she prepares to go on a journey with the king).

What I know of the current situation of the dreamer I have presented in the form of her conscious thought—as the most obvious meaning of the dream and with her subsequent full consent. This is, as it were, the uppermost layer of her recent fantasy life, whose contents I would hardly expect her to reveal directly.

These ambitious and erotic daydreams owe their nearly complete representation in the dream content to what Freud calls the *secondary elaboration* of the dream material, which has the tendency "to approximate the dream to the image of a comprehensible experience"; the various results of this secondary elaboration now present themselves to superficial observation as the façade of the dream.[30]

Through this achievement of dream work, dreams

> often arise which, to superficial observation, may seem absolutely logical and accurate … These dreams have undergone the most penetrating reprocessing by the mental function that is similar to waking thought; they seem to have a meaning, but this meaning is very far removed from the true meaning of the dream … These are dreams which have already been interpreted, as it were, before we interpret them while awake.
>
> (Freud, 1909a, p. 303)

We have been warned against being satisfied with such all too obvious and straightforward interpretations, yet we may expect that a dream that so clearly reveals the carefully kept secret of erotic daydreams does so only to conceal other wish fantasies still less capable of direct expression.

The frankness with which such a dream appears and its formally and logically impeccable presentation are intended to charm the critical faculty of consciousness into abandoning all further inquiry into a possible deeper meaning for the "already meaningful dream."[31]

If one does not allow oneself to be deceived by the well-constructed façade of the dream and its apparently satisfactory explanation, one can discover, with some certainty, behind the ambitious fantasy regarding a position and the erotic marriage fantasy—from isolated hints, all too clear in the manifest dream content—a more deeply buried sexual "hotel fantasy."[8]

The large elegant house with the many variously decorated rooms points directly to the hotel, a place which, as is well known, intensively occupies the fantasy of young women living in a big city. The hotel room is, in fact, a place forbidden to young women, and the bird scene there, described in detail, indicates the reason for this prohibition in language quite unambiguous for a dream.[21]

This fantasy is completed by the slim young man (tutor) who is described through ambiguous turns of phrase as forcing his way into the room, and also by the chambermaid who locks and unlocks the door and receives a reward (in Vienna 20 kreuzers—10 kreuzers per person); the fantasy appropriately ends with a scene of washing up (wash basin, mirror).[8a]

Besides the employment fantasy and the marriage fantasy, belonging to the dreamer's conscious thought and clearly revealed by the manifest dream content, and the more subtly indicated hotel fantasy, arising from the preconscious, this unusually transparent dream reveals a very deeply entrenched unconscious fantasy, actually responsible for the formation of the dream.

Setting aside the meaning of the dream as we have worked it out so far, we must make use of the previously mentioned abbreviated technique which, by translating certain typical symbols universal in human beings, reveals the unconscious sources of the dream in the most direct way.

One of the most reliable keys to symbolism shows that even the choice of the highly elegant milieu, a milieu making possible the most complete fulfilment of the dreamer's ambitious wishes, is more deeply determined.

From *The Interpretation of Dreams*, we know that "the emperor and empress (king and queen) in general actually represent the parents of the dreamer" (Freud, 1909a, p. 200); we have also found confirmation for this in the fantasy life of entire peoples through an age-old mythic tradition recurring among all cultured peoples (Rank, 1909).

In the dream presented above, it accords well with the mother character of the queen that she, in comparison to the daughter, is depicted as an older and strict lady to whose will the child must unconditionally submit; the beating scene, which does not at all fit with the relationship to an employee, directly supplies a reference to the mother.

Less clear is the identification of the king with the father, although we are accustomed from psychoanalyses to take such mutual erotic feelings as are implied in the dream as the typical relationship between a loving father and his little daughter who has matured early and is in need of affection (cf. Freud, 1905 ff.—typical in this respect).

Beneath this dream, then, would lie the typical incest fantasy discovered by Freud (1909a, p. 180 ff.; 1910a, p. 64 ff.; 1909b), which reveals itself more and more clearly as the actual "core complex of the neuroses" (cf. Freud, 1909c, p. 394: footnote), but which normally also decisively determines the subsequent erotic and social relationships of human beings later in life (cf. Jung, 1909, p. 155 ff.).

We may assume that this infantile constellation of affection for the father and a feeling of competition from the mother was originally very intense, and that it has had a lasting influence on our dreamer; our assumptions are supported by the central position of such a constellation in this dream and by the unusually affective emphasis upon it.

With the uncovering of this childhood fantasy—one that is very deeply anchored in the unconscious and is the real creator of the dream—the previously emphasised stratification of the various layers of imagery, all of unequal value, becomes obvious.

We immediately recognise, for example, that the choice of the royal milieu does not spring from the daydream, as do other elements of the conscious employment fantasy, but from the infantile constellation of complexes.

Yet, at the same time, we notice that this royal milieu could appear in the dream content only because it partially corresponds with the conscious daydreams tending toward a maximally elegant milieu.[17] In the same way, the beating scene could be of infantile origin, and its inclusion in the dream content could similarly be due to the fact that it relates figuratively to submissiveness toward an employer. [*In her account of the dream, the dreamer subsequently refers to the queen as "the lady."*]

The hand kissing may serve as a combining element, belonging both to the recent and to the infantile situation. [*This temporary assumption is later fully confirmed by the dreamer.*] Similar overlaps, in essential points, of the recent (conscious) and infantile (unconscious) fantasies, as well as isolated characteristic deviations from this parallelism, can be recognised behind the mixed person who allows us to identify the father (the king) with various male employers, for example, the surprise at the washing scene, a scene which is inevitable in the case of the father, and which is nearly inevitable in an employer's home as well. [*This temporary assumption is later fully confirmed by the dreamer.*]

Thus individual situations in the dream may be explained as "concealing and combining images" (Freud, 1909a, p. 233), for example, the rooms do not belong to the marriage fantasy or hotel fantasy alone, but also suggest the parents' home (the royal palace) as it may have seemed to the dreamer, through childish amelioration, when she was a girl.

The unusual leave-taking ceremony seems most alien to the waking thoughts of the dreamer, but one of its elements may make it comprehensible—the very one that seems to fit least with an infantile explanation of this whole scene. It is the action of the mother that contradicts her character, consistently described as strict: after the beating, she not only forgives her daughter through the hand kissing, but also grants her a reward that actually involves permission to do what is usually forbidden.

This conflicts with our attempted interpretation, which showed the mother precisely as an impediment to the forbidden (affection for the father). In such a confusing situation, dream theory provides a proven tool which should never be left untried in such cases. This is the technique of reading backwards such a constituent of the manifest dream content that offers stubborn resistance to interpretation. The connection often becomes immediately clear (cf. the first dream in Freud, 1905, noticeably similar both in content and form).

If we apply this empirically discovered rule to the detail under discussion, through "inversion of time and content" in the manifest text, we can reconstruct the previous stage in the dream thought approximately as follows: "I entered a forbidden room, and as a punishment (in the dream a reward) I was whipped by my mother with a switch, after which I asked her to forgive me." From this sensible rearrangement, one could conclude that this dream situation reproduces a childhood scene in which the dreamer, because she had done something forbidden, might have been severely punished by her mother.

But in this form, the thought is too clear and thus too painful. Through inversion to the opposite, both of these offensive traits are eliminated. Thus the inversion serves first of all to emphasise wish-fulfilment with respect to a certain element in the dream thought, and it is characteristic of the functioning of dreams that the dreamer receives as a reward precisely what she deserved punishment for in her original dream thoughts.

In the service of censorship, inversion is thus especially valuable since it produces so much distortion of the material that it effectively paralyses the understanding of the dream.

The easy solution of this challenging inversion prepares us to consider that other elements belonging to this scene might also have undergone such a transformation.[42a]

In the dream, the punishment for violation of the prohibition precedes the departure of the queen (mother). From the dreamer's life, we know that it was really she who left her parents' home to escape the all too strict supervision by her mother, and we may conclude from the inversion of this circumstance in the dream that she herself would have preferred to see the departure of her strict mother from her father's home.

But we have good reason to assume that this wish for the removal of the mother, who was perceived only as disturbing, had been aroused in her earlier as a child, given the child's one-sided erotic attitude—and that this wish might then have taken as its goal the permanent removal of the mother.[1]

The journey complex too, with its infantile secondary meaning of death (departure), is only permitted to enter the dream because it can be linked to a current thought. Just as she previously left her parents' home, the dreamer must again leave her current residence and go out into the world to earn a living.

If one reads the opening of the dream in its original meaning, the opposite of the text above, it begins with a reproach toward the mother, who drove her daughter from the home through her excessive strictness. "I had to go away from the child to take leave of her" would now mean: "When I took leave of my mother (left home) I had to go to the child, i.e. earn my living as a governess. But things are not going as badly for me as my mother might wish. Instead, I am much better off than at home: I am in a royal palace."

But we have learned to understand the royal palace as the infantile replacement for the parents' home, and in this sense, the beginning of the dream expresses regret that she had not been better off at home, in both the social and erotic senses.

In the distorted dream text, one can clearly hear her disappointment concerning the strict attitude of her mother—"I thought I would be well off here, and now she's beating me"—and also her regret at the loss of her mother's former embraces—"I had to take leave of her (take leave of her love) when I ceased to be a child" ("I had to go away from the child to take leave of her").

The inversion in the dream thus makes it possible to blame the mother for all the ill fortune and to take revenge on her in the form of vengeful thoughts.

"'If it had only been the other way around!' is often the best expression of the ego's attitude toward a painful memory" (Freud, 1909a, p. 238). "If my mother had gone away instead of me, if she had died instead of my father, then I wouldn't need to earn my living as a governess (employment fantasy). Instead, I could long ago have been happily married" (i.e. with the father (king): infantile marriage fantasy). [*Consciously, she expresses this thought in her feeling that everything would have been quite different, and of course happier, if her father were still alive.*]

The source of such a childish wish for the death of the same-sex parent is regularly shown to be the longing for the completely undisturbed, sole possession of the better beloved, opposite-sex parent. (Information on the origin and nature of such infantile wishes is provided in Freud, 1909a, p. 176; 1909b.)

Furthermore, in this case, the dreamer's incredulous surprise at the news of the king's departure guarantees to us that she wished her mother away only so as to be alone with her father.[2]

Such a strong expression of the parent complex is only possible on the basis of an intensive erotic feeling that is awakened early; behind the prohibition which was violated in childhood and which led to punishment, this insight leads us to suspect an offence in the sphere of erotic experience, or at least to derive the guilty feeling in the dream thoughts, which is expressed in the punishment scene, from erotic sources.

Let us see the extent to which the dream content justifies such a supposition. There the forbidden thing is a Chinese lilac room, whose sexual meaning has already been revealed by its connection with the hotel fantasy. This, so to speak, full sexual meaning does not correspond to the suspected infantile one, but we might again pursue that infantile meaning through dream symbolism, which teaches us that in a dream, rooms (*Zimmer*) mostly signify women (*Frauenzimmer*).

The description of their various exits and entrances does not contradict this interpretation. The dream of going through a sequence of rooms is actually a dream of a brothel or harem (Freud, 1909a, p. 200).

If the dream had been dreamt by a man, we would not hesitate for a moment to accept this interpretation. But what can women's rooms (*Frauenzimmer*) mean in the case of a thoroughly feminine young woman in whom there is no reason whatsoever to assume a homosexual orientation?

It will satisfy the critical reader, who by now has become impatient, and it was also welcome to the analyst, that the interpretation of this dream—ideal since it could be interpreted without recourse to other information—was interrupted by the unsuspecting dreamer's surprising comment that the dream was not yet over, but continued into a second "not nearly so pretty or interesting part."

This announcement, expressed with reservations leading one to infer a secret resistance to relating this part, may make one curious about the following dream narration, which ensued after some resistance and with the help of written notes.

Part 2

I was at home, in my hometown, and went out for a walk in the fields, where I cut off some beautiful ears of barley and rye. [*Upon repetition: "I thought to myself 'I won't tear them off.' Instead, I cut them off with a knife I had with me."*] [*Later: "I looked down toward the train station and saw a young man, H., approaching. I looked to see whether he was actually coming up the road, but he just remained in the same spot. Then I noticed a beautiful field of beets, with beautiful large leaves."*]

I found it strange that the barley was ripe first, and then the rye, since otherwise it's the reverse, of course. Also, the ears struck me as especially beautiful, full, and ripe. I carried the cut ears in my apron so that no one would reveal what I had done, and headed for home.

I went past the mill; close by, a childhood friend, Z., emerged from the public baths and tipped his hat to me. He walked to the field where I had just been, and I wanted to avoid his speaking to me because I thought: "He will inspect the crops and will see that I've cut the ears." I headed for home. [*On repetition: "The ground was suddenly muddy, which surprised me since it had not rained in the meantime."*]

I met a young woman, A., who was standing before her door. [*On repetition: "She had a dog with her."*] She was holding something black in her hand—a jar of plum jam, or something similar. She asked: "Where have you been?" "I've been for a walk," I said.

Then she saw the ears of grain protruding from my apron, and I was displeased that she had noticed. She said: "I suppose you've cut them off for your landlady's chickens." I said: "Yes." Close by stood another classmate, B. The first young woman, A., said: "She also came here from Vienna." I said: "I see!" Then A. said she wouldn't speak to B., and I answered: "I'm also angry with her."

A. walked with me for a while, and we passed B., who stopped me and asked: "Where have you been?" [*Later: "While we were talking together, A. crouched down by the gate of her house, stirring about with a stick (or brush) on the ground and acting as though she wasn't listening to me."*]

I said: "I was taking a walk." "What have you got in your apron?" "Ears of grain." "So the crop was already cut down?" "Yes." "So you gathered them after the reaping?" I said, "Yes" because I didn't want to admit that I had cut them off myself.

She had some needlework in her hand, and through the gate, which stood open, I saw her garden, which attracted me very much. Then she asked me if I would like to come in. I said: "Yes, but I must first take the ears of grain home."⁵

The landlady was delighted when I gave them to her and declared that the hens would lay fine eggs now. Then I was with my classmate B. in her house: we were naked and loved each other …

It may initially appear that this second dream, separated in time from the first dream, shows no relationship to the first one in terms of content. But a closer examination of its manifest content indicates certain superficial parallels. Thus, given the regular functioning of dreams, we may expect deeper material connections.

The dreamer's more precise portrayal of individual details already leads us to recognise that in the two dreams the same material is presented from different points of view. To the man washing at the sink in the first dream corresponds the young man emerging from the public baths in the second dream. The hens in the second dream are analogous to the bird in the first dream. In both dreams, the entrancing garden plays a role. The bundle of ears in the apron [*also anticipated in the first dream in the chambermaid's white apron*] corresponds to the mother's instrument of punishment in the first dream, which the dreamer describes as a bundle of birch switches such as, according to an old folk-custom, *Krampus* brings to naughty children. Finally, one notices the remarkably similar structures and a certain stereotyped form of dialogue in both dreams. [*In the first dream, the king "said he was going away. I said in amazement: 'So, you're going away?' 'Yes,' he said, 'I'm going away.'" In the second dream, friend A. asks: "Where have you been?" The dreamer responds: "I was taking a walk," which B. repeats almost word for word.*] Based on these external correspondences, the second dream would serve to affirm and further develop the interpretation assumed for the first dream, but it would be preferable to obtain direct proofs of the hypothesised interpretation of the first dream—an interpretation I take as the foundation for further analytical work.

With this aim, I explained to the dreamer how king and queen represent father and mother. She responded: "That's certainly possible, for the queen in the dream had the same eye colour and hair colour as my mother, and an elderly face like hers, but the facial features were not those of my mother." I replied that the features were probably combined from recollections of various mistresses, which she also admitted was "possible."[35] [*At the beginning of Part 1, the dreamer, on repetition, refers to the queen as "the lady."*]

The same would hold for the king, who had black hair and a black moustache like the father, who was considered a handsome man, and who had died rather young (ten years earlier).

Her relationship to her father and mother as she now described it, having been asked—though not suspecting that she was supplying an important contribution to the interpretation of the dream—also provides proof of our conception.

In childhood, she clung to her father with unusual affection, and still thinks of him with all too painful emotion: she feels that things would be quite different, were her father still living. For as long as she could remember, she had never been on good terms with her mother, and this strained relationship became more acute after her father's death and her mother's remarriage, which followed soon after: the dreamer was angry with her mother for a whole year (during this time, she lived with an aunt), and then she left her parents' home for good. We thus find full confirmation of the hypothesised Oedipus complex *feminini generis*, as the Greek legend of Electra depicts it with blunt clarity.

Encouraged by this success, I attempted to enlighten the dreamer about the symbolism of the lilac room, adding that this was confirmed beyond all doubt by the frankness of the second dream. It was already pointed out[35] how characteristic are the responses to connections of this kind, and the psychoanalyst is accustomed to hearing in the initial firm "no" only the drowning out of an unconscious "yes."

The dreamer dismissed the explanation of the rooms as women as a bad joke; she rejected it in a calm way, which one would not be justified in interpreting as unconscious agreement. I then tried to explain to her that the second dream indeed represents the rooms of the first dream as women. Then she became indignant and said in a tone intended to put an end to the discussion: "My goodness! As far as I'm concerned, they may be images of men (*Mannsbilder*)."

This remark, out of place as it is, is the more striking as it seems not at all suited to settling the discussion, and stands in disturbing contrast with the otherwise carefully chosen words of the dreamer. I immediately recalled a similar wordplay (*Frauenzimmer: "women" or "women's room(s)"—Weibsbilder: "women" or "images of women"*) from *Fragment of an Analysis of Hysteria* (Freud, 1905), and understood the true sense of her utterance, which had actually been intended to put an end to the discussion.

Indeed, it is a confirmation of the interpretation in a form the unconscious can manage. Figuratively speaking, it is as if her unconscious were crying out over her conscious denial: "O yes, I am quite capable of using such ambiguous compound words." Freud has designated such expressions as an unconscious, indirect "yes": no other "yes" (a direct "yes") will be heard from the unconscious.

Since I did not explain to the dreamer the meaning of this unconscious confirmation, she believed I had renounced the interpretation equating rooms with women. She expressed an idea she found decisive for explaining the forbidden room: on the morning after the dream, she was immediately struck by its similarity to the fairy tale *Bluebeard*.

There too, among several permitted rooms, one room is forbidden; there too, feminine curiosity in violating the prohibition is severely punished. This reminiscence initially convinces us that we were correct in reading the opening scene of the dream in reverse (first the violation of the prohibition and then the punishment), but it also expresses quite new interpretive material in symbolic language that cannot be misunderstood.

This symbolic language is not limited to dreams, but belongs generally to unconscious thought, especially that of the common people. In folklore, myths, legends, figures of speech, proverbs, and popular jokes of a nation, it is more complete than in dreams (Freud, 1909a, p. 199). (Cf. especially Riklin, 1908.)

The fairy tale *Bluebeard* centres on opening a forbidden door, whose key is entrusted to the young woman as a test of her resolve. The basic idea of many permitted doors and one forbidden door recurs many times and with different introductions, as in the fairy tale *Fitcher's Bird* (Grimm and Grimm, 1885, Nr. 46) and in *A Child of Saint Mary* (Grimm and Grimm, 1885, Nr. 3). Freud notes that "the opening of closed doors is one of the most common sexual symbols" (1909a, p. 197). Indeed, it is closely connected with the symbolism of the room "since it cannot be insignificant whether a woman's room (*Frauenzimmer*) is open or shut" (p. 197). "It is also clear which 'key' opens the door in this case" (Freud, 1905).[3] [*We shall note here the sexual-symbolic meaning of the unlocking scene in the first dream, which underlies the erotically depicted hotel fantasy.*]

From a psychological examination of fairy tales, one now gains the impression that this clearly sexual symbolism of dreams and popular humour in fairy tales, intended as they are for children, is applied, as it were, in an autoerotic sense corresponding to infantile sexual feelings, and relates to masturbation, the sexual activity forbidden to children.

In due course, in the discussion of a different connection, the current impression of arbitrariness will be eliminated. Here, we will merely point out that quite consistently corresponding to this sexual-symbolic meaning, these stories dealing with the forbidden opening of a closed door introduce a young woman as the guilty trespasser.

Stekel, in a short essay, "The Symbolism of Fairy Tales" (1908a), was able to explain the story of *Fitcher's Bird* as a means of violating the prohibition on masturbation. In a psychologically more accurate but also somewhat more sublimated form, *A Child of Saint Mary* describes this most serious of infantile offences with its consequences, mental (anxiety) and physical (dumbness, upward displacement).[22] [The Virgin Mary transports the three-year-old girl to heaven (Translator's Note).]

If we may conclude from the fairy tale symbolism of the first dream— and the dreamer's recollection of *Bluebeard*, which pointed us in this direction—that the forbidden entrance into the closed room has such a meaning stretching back into childhood, it is the second dream which again shows this assumption to be well founded.

In the second dream, the masturbation complex is also expressed, and far more clearly. The symbolism of forcing one's way into a closed room more closely approaches the popular meaning (virginity), but the fantasy symbolically expressed in the plucking of ears of grain has an undoubtedly masturbatory sense. [*The needlework in the second dream also hints at masturbation*, cf. Stekel, 1908b, p. 223.]

There is an expression—used by all children and popular with adults as well—for the act of masturbation: *sich einen ausreissen* "to pull one out" or *sich einen herunterreissen* "to pull one down" (Freud, 1909a, p. 195).

When dreams involve tearing off flowers, blossoms, branches, fruits, etc., one can safely assume this infantile sexual meaning (cf. "The Flower Dream" in Freud, 1909a, p. 2), indicated with extreme clarity by the sexual connotation of these elements (flower, blossom, fruit, etc.). The fact that the dream involves ears of grain must have a special significance, which we shall subsequently pursue.

I next had the dreamer depict in great detail the scene involving the ears of grain, though I did not discuss their sexual sense with her. It was at this point that she produced the previously cited comment about the young man she saw coming up from the train station, but who then seemed to remain on the same spot. ["*While we were talking together, A. crouched down by the gate of her house, stirring about with a stick (or brush) on the ground and acting as though she wasn't listening to me.*"]

Then she continued: "I paid him no more attention. Meanwhile, it was the beautiful field of grain I had noticed that attracted my interest. I first looked in all directions to see whether anyone was watching, and then I surreptitiously cut off the ears.[9] I was afraid someone might see me and reveal what I had done, for in the dream all of this was forbidden." (Cf. the similar depiction of the state of anxiety in *A Child of Saint Mary.*)

I asked her why she had placed the ears of grain in her apron. "I didn't want anyone to see what I had done, but (in the dream) I kept meeting people; everyone noticed that I had ears of grain in my apron though they were not yet ripe." This affect of anxiety, by no means corresponding to the dream content,[10] unambiguously marks this forbidden and secretly executed activity as sexual, and makes its sexual-symbolic guise comprehensible as a consequence of repression.

In this deeper layer of dream meaning, we will need to deal with the dreamer's surprise at the early and highly noticeable ripeness of the barley, contrasting with the still unripe rye, as a contrast between full sexual maturity and early maturity (sexual immaturity), probably relating to the dreamer herself (masturbation, parent complex).[10a] Further investigation of the meaning of these two species of grain and of the source of the ears provides a wealth of preconscious material which will take us further in the interpretation of the second dream.

In the summer preceding this dream, dreamt in December, the dreamer was visiting her hometown after an absence of many years; the beginning of the second dream resembles a conscious report about this. She had really gone for a walk among the fields, something she had especially enjoyed as a child and as a young woman, and had admired the beautiful and full grain. But besides these pleasant and sentimental childhood memories, the short visit to her hometown caused her a series of painful feelings, produced especially upon seeing her mother, so long estranged from her, and upon seeing a suitor favoured by her mother as a match for the dreamer; she had previously been as good as engaged to him, but had meanwhile broken away from him within herself, without clarifying this to anyone.

She had strongly wished to avoid seeing this young man (designated as H.); in the dream, this wish is associated with another childhood friend, Z. In reality, her mother's active gossiping made it impossible to avoid the encounter. One day when the dreamer was walking down the path she had so often taken between the fields—a path also seen in the dream—her mother sent her fiancé after her, as he had been granted a few days of military leave.

Surprised by a sudden rain (in the dream the ground suddenly became muddy, though it had not rained), she ran to the nearby house of a woman she knew, and later, while walking home, noticed a young man coming up the road toward her from the train station. He seemed familiar, though she could not definitively place him. As he drew closer, she recognised him as her fiancé and was painfully embarrassed, unsure of how to act toward him and of how he would act toward her.

Thus, like the beginning of the dream, the dreamer's comments report real experiences, though corrected as she would wish, so that H. remained on the same spot, and did not approach her.[12]

The sudden transition in the scenery of the dream to the field of grain suggests that she wished to avoid the encounter because she was keeping a secret from her fiancé (the severed ears of grain in the dream). Her fear that the secret could be discovered by her childhood friend Z., who appears later and whom we have already seen in place of H.,[11] confirms the causal relationship described above.

Evidence is also provided by the fact that the words of the young women in the dream, which relate to the discovery of the secret, derive in part from the actual conversation with the dreamer's fiancé; other portions derive from conversations the dreamer happened to overhear during her visit to her hometown, or from her own words (Freud, 1909a, p. 256).[13]

The beginning of the second dream reproduces the summer visit to the young woman's hometown—a visit so significant in her mental life—and the scene with the young man who had been engaged to her sparks memories of the years she had spent there as a girl, but the last part of the dream, which includes her female schoolmates and hints at childhood eroticism, seems to contain infantile material.

It is probably the case that the visit at home, with its various impressions, reactivated the entire story of her childhood, which now finds expression in the dream. Correspondingly, in the second dream too, we recognise the layering of various levels of material that overlap in specific and significant nodal points and, through an obvious parallelism, correspond to the fantasies given expression in the first dream. Thus, the uppermost level of material in the second dream—the level reproducing the summer visit—is the complement and simultaneously the ideal fulfilment (royal palace) of the employment fantasy in the first dream.

Indeed, it shows the dreamer removed from her present, undecided position in life and living carefree in her parents' home, taking a walk among the fields, just as she had done in the previous summer (and as a child). Similarly, the reminiscence of her engagement in the second dream hints that she should renounce her current elevated and uncertain marriage plans and content herself to live in modest surroundings with a quiet happiness.

But just as in the first dream, here again barriers arise, and it is only the deepest unconscious-infantile layer of the dream that offers her the satisfaction—sought in vain both in her current life and in the first dream—that she experienced as a child. Now, once again, she can do what is forbidden (cut off ears of grain) without being punished.

What allows the ears of grain to function in the dream as a substitute for the forbidden act, which must be kept secret, is the fact that they are able to reach through all the levels of the dream with an alternating meaning, which can actually connect them. [*It should be noted that the dreamer supported her auspicious interpretation of the dream with this detail, referring to the biblical pharaoh's dream of the seven full and seven thin ears of grain.*]

First, on the uppermost level, as a recollection of the beauty of the previous summer, they have for the enraptured young women an aesthetic and sentimental meaning. Among these beautiful fields of grain, though, as a part of her summer visit, she also walked with her fiancé, just as she had done when she still felt affection for him.

Although they had an unpleasant argument during the walk, things had been more pleasant in earlier years: they were in love and had first exchanged kisses on this path. Here, as a sort of ironic justification, the dreamer wove in the expression, often jokingly transformed: "No one can refuse an honourable kiss" ("*Einen Kuss in Ehren kann niemand verwehren*"). She then added, with clear reference to the cited expression: "We really did kiss among the ears of grain" ("*Wir haben uns auch wirklich in Ähren geküsst*"). [German *Ehren* "honours" and *Ähren* "ears of grain" are homophones (Translator's Note).]

We note here that the dreamer did not recall this play on words merely by chance. Rather, the play on words establishes a superficial but preformed bridge between the two dreams. To the ears of grain correspond the honours granted the dreamer in the royal palace (the honour of entering the forbidden room).

In the interpretation of dreams and in the resolution of neurotic symptoms these superficial associations, so-called word bridges, have a function that should not be underestimated.

Indeed, psychoanalytic research has shown that "in such cases, under the pressure of censorship, there occurs a shift from a normal, serious association to a superficial, seemingly absurd one. In the interpretation of dreams, since we are aware of such shifts, we also rely without hesitation on the superficial associations." For "whenever one mental element is connected with another through an offensive and superficial association, there exists also an inoffensive and deeper connection between the two that is subject to the resistance effected by censorship" (Freud, 1909a, p. 326).

In our case, the play on words ceases to seem forced, since in this sense the popular joke has already done its work, allowing us to rely on this word bridge with a greater degree of security.[33] The deeper and serious connection is easily revealed if we recall the sexual-symbolic meaning of tearing off ears of grain; the concept of honour gains the special sense of sexual honour apparently sullied by infantile sexual activity.

Now we surmise what the dreamer wishes to keep secret from her fiancé and from Z., who is identified with him. Just as she must have feared as a child that one might suspect her masturbatory activity, she now fears it will be discovered that she has, as it is expressed in the dream, broken off the ears of grain (*Ähren*), that is, her honour (*Ehre*).[23]

In the context of her female classmates, we can assume that this fear relates in the unconscious to masturbation, and that in the context of her fiancé, it is intended to express the additional meaning of doubts about her virginity.[12a] (As it turns out, a man with whom she had previously had a relationship, had "cut off her honour.") Thus, all the dream elements belonging to the complex of the ears of grain are to be understood in a doubly symbolic sense, and also with a sort of allegorical meaning (honour). In this context, wanting to hide something and fear of discovery become meaningful.

The recognition that the second dream is a reproduction of and a reaction to the recent conflicts reactivated during the summer visit suggests the need to investigate the immediate recent factors giving rise to the entire dream.

The structure and tendency of the first dream seemed so transparent to us that we initially believed we could dispense with the material of those recent factors giving rise to the dream—the material most easily accessible to the dreamer.

Given that the summer visit, six months beforehand, presented itself as the factor directly producing the second dream—a visit one cannot designate as a "recent factor" in the sense of dream theory—we must investigate, by examining the first dream, the connections to direct experiences of the day that gave rise to the entire dream sequence. We can expect that the uncovering of these recent dream sources will give us access to further dream thoughts.

An inquiry about this revealed the following experiences of the previous day that are connected with the dream. The younger boy in the family in whose home the dreamer was living at the time of the dream had received a siskin [a small finch that has a distinctly forked tail and a long narrow bill (Translator's Note)] as a gift from a friend, which the young woman, a fanatical animal lover, sometimes held and kissed.

She then mentioned that in Vienna, in the Imperial Zoo at Schönbrunn, she had seen colourful parrots with red, blue, green, and yellow feathers, which she liked so much that she had already been wishing for such a bird for some time (wish!). Most of all, she liked a beautiful red bird (of a single colour). [*At the same time, she also dreamt of three pink parrots; their feathers bore patterns in a Chinese style, and in her dream she wished to have one of them.*]

It becomes immediately clear that the fantastic purple bird with the long tail seen in the dream derives from impressions gained at the zoo and from the conversation about them on the previous day, though the bird, as we were able to determine, is used in the dreamer's unconscious dream thoughts with sexual-symbolic meaning.

Furthermore, on the previous day, the dreamer had read in a family magazine a report on the life, customs, and clothing of the Chinese; among other factors, this report undoubtedly determined the Chinese attire of the queen. Finally, on the evening prior to the dream she had had a conversation with a young man, a friend of hers, in which they discussed the curious manner of greeting of the Eskimos; the young man had stated that for people like the two of them, after rubbing noses, it would be much more natural to proceed directly to contact with the lips.

Also in the dream content, the unusual greeting ceremony strikes me as strange. The dreamer must touch the floor with her nose, and the erotic reference made by her male friend prepares us to acknowledge that behind the prostrate position in the dream a sexual-symbolic meaning may lie hidden.[27]

According to Freud (1909a, p. 125), these generally indifferent causal factors from daily experience are meaningfully used in the dream content in that they are a shifted substitute for important impressions that are mentally fully valued, and which in a deeper layer of mental life correspond to logically well-ordered and coherent trains of thought.

Dream work is only able to present this material by joining these seemingly disparate elements as a unity. In this case, it is especially fortunate that such a connective element, which it is usually the task of the dream work to produce with greater or lesser success, is already provided in waking thought.

Indeed, the dream was dreamt one night before the eve of Saint Nicholas Day (6 December), a celebration that plays its double role (reward or punishment) not only in the nursery, but also among adults, who may enjoy giving each other gifts or teasing each other with amusing threats.

It is understandable that this upcoming occasion for the giving of gifts awakened in the dreamer a number of wishes (pink parrot) and expectations, two of which are of special interest to us.

On the previous Easter, she had unexpectedly received from her mother, with whom she is not on the best of terms, the gift of a pink nightgown; she considered this a favourable omen for her upcoming summer visit. While at her mother's home, she had then hinted that she would also like another nightgown with Turkish (or Chinese) patterns. Indeed, she was told that it would be sent for Christmas. At that time, she learned that in lieu of the pink nightgown, it had originally been intended that she receive one with purple polka-dots, but that her sister had objected to its purchase.[1a]

Here, we find another determining factor for the Chinese gown in the dream, and another sense arises also for the vibrant colours of the rooms, one that stands in a certain harmony with their symbolic meaning (women's rooms, nightgowns).[7]

The dreamer had already hoped to receive the promised Turkish nightgown on Saint Nicholas Day, but was unsure whether this expectation would be fulfilled since she had previously departed from her mother without being fully reconciled; the fact that her mother had not written to her for a long time revealed her embittered mood.

Thus it was with some doubts but also a certain excitement, in which was concentrated her entire ambiguous relationship with her mother, that she awaited this occasion for gift-giving—the first that had presented itself to her mother since the daughter's departure.

On the other hand, she admits that she hoped to receive at least a birch switch from the young man with whom she had had the conversation about the Eskimos, and whose relationship with her excluded presenting her with expensive or meaningful gifts; such a switch is given as a warning to naughty children, and she had once received one from one of her admirers.

In the dream, her mother is wearing a Chinese (or Turkish) gown and also holds a birch switch in her hand, and thus punishes the daughter doubly: by withholding gifts and by beating her. The dream thus reveals to us that the dreamer's unconscious, in contrast to her conscious hopes, was not afraid she would not receive the gift, but that a secret sense of guilt suggested to her that she was more deserving of punishment than of reward (cf. the inversion of wishes in the dream).[15]

The dreamer was immediately able to answer inquiries about this sense of guilt in a fully sufficient manner. At the time of her departure the preceding summer, she was accompanied to the train station by her mother and sister, where she kept delaying the embarrassing moment of leave-taking, always referring to the long time remaining before the departure of the train.

She continued in this way until the train actually arrived and there was no more time to say goodbye. She kissed her mother hastily on the hand and stepped onto the already departing train. She had thus achieved what she hoped for—namely, the avoidance of the farewell kiss, which she was supposedly "embarrassed" to give her mother.

We now see in what a richly meaningful way the dream is constructed. It is not only for resisting the appropriate leave-taking that she is punished by her mother. Indeed, through the birch switch and the Chinese gown, the dream also hints that the dreamer, due to the inappropriate manner of her departure, fears she will be punished by her mother rather than receiving a Saint Nicholas Day gift from her—as she may also have feared as a child.[32]

It would thus be appropriate to interpret this scene, characterised by mysterious images, as follows: in the dream, the mother demands the leave-taking owed her but withheld from her. She says, as it were, since you did not wish to depart appropriately ("I didn't want to do so"), I'll keep the nightgown for myself, and instead of the nightgown, you'll get a beating (for Saint Nicholas Day) unless you now make amends for your previous inappropriate behaviour.

Thus, the dreamer carries the poorly executed leave-taking over into the dream, under pressure from her mother and with unmistakable ironic exaggeration, as if she wished to say: "It seems one must bow before you and throw oneself to the ground as if you were the queen of China."[3]

On the other hand, this exaggerated devotion can be interpreted as an intentional belated compensation, intended to effect a quick reconciliation with her mother before the eve of Saint Nicholas Day. It is notable that this compensation, contrary to what we would expect, is not brought about through a kiss, previously denied, but rather, as the dreamer later clarified, through a doubling of the kiss on the hand (before and after the beating).

As suggested earlier, the repetition of this demonstration of respect serves to identify various mistresses with the mother, and the fact that even in the dream the actual "honourable kiss" is avoided reveals the full effect of the previously noted ambivalent emotions associated with the mother, which doubtless arise from the childhood constellation: immense respect, on the one hand, and ironic ridicule, on the other.

First of all, it is due to exaggerated respect that she does not kiss her mother on the mouth: such a greeting by a subordinate person toward the mistress would of course be inappropriate. The failure to kiss her on the mouth is also associated with respect for a figuratively suggested command of the mother: "Since you did not wish to kiss me, then, as punishment, you must now kiss the ground."

In this punishing manner of greeting, though, ridicule of the mother's strictness also breaks through. It is as if the young woman, like a child, were pointing to her nose and crying out: "Indeed, there (by the nose) I will not kiss you!" (cf. the Eskimo greeting).[18] [*Pointing to the nose is an expression of ridicule to which, affectively, she now spontaneously takes recourse.*]

Thus, in the recent fantasy about Saint Nicholas Day, we find justification for the reversal in this scene of the dream. Indeed, this thought underlies it: "Oh, if I had departed appropriately at that time, things would be reversed; now I would be able to expect a gift rather than a punishment."

Indeed, the dream shows her this wish fulfilled: things are reversed. She has really departed in a manner completely satisfactory to her mother, thus deservedly receiving the longed-for reward (purple room).[15]

With this, we might have gained an entirely sufficient interpretation of the apparently absurd greeting scene, yet we have repeatedly been pushed toward the assumption that the beating scene also has infantile roots.

According to the theory of dreams, we must also assume that neither the recent fantasy about Saint Nicholas Day nor the scene of leave-taking from the mother, connected as they are in her thoughts and certainly based on infantile models, would have sufficed to produce a dream if infantile, unconscious impressions and experiences had not found secret expression in the dream.

In the manifest content of every dream, we expect to find a connection with recent experience, but in the latent content a connection with earliest experience (Freud, 1909a, p. 1).

If we could show that the beating scene had really been experienced, or at least that the infantile sense of guilt underlying it was founded in reality, we would have found, as required by dream theory, the infantile model of the fantasised dream situation and thus direct access to the infantile sources of the dream (Freud, 1905, p. 79, footnote).

When asked whether she recalled an especially memorable scene of beating from childhood, the dreamer remembered only the last time she was beaten, at the age of fourteen (the year of her father's death and her last year of school).[45a]

For telling a lie, her mother had beaten her with a switch, a switch used exclusively for this purpose, which leads me to conclude that it must have been used more often than the young woman was willing to admit.

A more detailed depiction of the beating she experienced and of the dream situation now yields a certain correlation between the two. This allows me to surmise how great a role in the formation of this dream scene was played by the young woman's actual previous experience. She indicated that in the dream she had approached the queen, who was sitting on a Chinese chest, and that she had kissed the queen's hand, whereupon she had been commanded to lie on the floor. She did not wish to do this since she found it "embarrassing," so initially she merely knelt.

Then the queen beat her in the face with the switch, whereupon the dreamer prostrated herself as described. However, she immediately stood up again and kissed the queen's hand again. During this scene, she was weeping and thinking to herself: "The things she demands of me! I must prostrate myself like a Chinese person (before the queen)."

In reality, when she believed she deserved a beating, she would actually kneel down before her mother and beg for forgiveness—an effort which, as seen in the dream, was usually in vain. Through these correspondences with reality, the beating scene in the dream shows its derivation from earlier scenes of beating actually experienced by the young woman, but it is actually the alterations that demonstrate the peculiar achievement of dream work—especially the formation of layers—in a characteristic way.

As they are taken into the dream content, real situations regularly undergo these alterations (Freud, 1909a, p. 139). Thus, when a bundle of switches appears in the dream rather than the single switch actually used by the mother, we already know that this transformation is derived from the opposing fantasy about Saint Nicholas Day, and is selected with reference to the sense of guilt associated with the bundle of grain ("tearing off").

From this association and from the sexual-symbolic sense of the "reward" inserted into the dream (the forbidden room), it would now be appropriate to identify masturbation as the source of this secret sense of guilt, and there is no doubt that the fear of discovery and punishment of this childhood fault (tearing off the ears of grain)—a fear which characterises the second dream—also plays a role in the sense of guilt evinced in the first dream.

But especially for the sense of guilt in the first dream, a deeper and more relevant source seems to present itself. Formally, the beating scene in the dream is a recapitulation of similar infantile situations, but in terms of its content, the scene is intimately connected with the scene of leave-taking at the train station. The beating scene in the dream provides an exaggerated correction of the leave-taking scene at the train station, but the affect of "embarrassment" associated with the mother, an affect shared by both scenes, is especially significant.

Just as the young woman was "embarrassed" in reality to give her mother a farewell kiss, she indicated that in the dream she had also been "embarrassed" to prostrate herself before her mother. But this affect of "needing to feel embarrassed" [*in the dream, we see the desired opposite: "being honoured"*][44] could, like the beating scene itself, derive from an infantile source, and we are already well prepared to find, as the source of the multiple distortions of the greeting scene, the strong repression of an especially offensive complex.

From isolated clues in the second dream, and from analogous experiences in other cases, we can with a certain degree of certainty identify this "embarrassing" activity also punished by the mother, given the content of the greeting scene.

Disregarding the already identified activity in the genital zone (masturbation), which indeed the dreamer recalled only from before puberty and later had to admit, and which, according to Freud, has its earlier infantile pre-history, we are dealing here mainly with an even earlier infantile source of pleasure from the erogenous zones.

This relates especially to the anal membranes and to the urethral meatus [the opening of the urethra, the point where urine exits the urethra in both sexes (Translator's Note)], whose erogenous function normally insures the excretory function of the infant, and whose later use as a source of pleasure leads to the childhood fault of uncleanliness, which is very strictly punished by parents and other caretakers.

When I wished to suggest to the dreamer that children are also very often punished for such persistent uncleanliness lasting up to a relatively advanced age, she interrupted me with a humorously presented thought that provides full confirmation for our understanding.

She said that the manner of punishment in the first dream reminded her of the way dogs are housebroken: one beats them and forces their nose down into their urine. I asked her whether she had also suffered from the childhood fault of wetting herself and had really been punished for it, but she claimed to remember such a situation with certainty only in the case of her brother.[36]

She said she remembered from when she was about eleven years old that her brother, about nine years old at the time, had been beaten for this. Indeed, she suddenly recalled the threat her mother had expressed toward her brother: "If you do that again, I'll push your nose down into it."

This feared punishment is thus the original, unconscious source of the strange greeting ceremony, whose preconscious meanings we were already able to demonstrate, and whose ultimate unconscious sense we shall soon discuss in detail.

After some persistent questioning, she admitted in regard to herself that she remembered only a single time she had wet the bed—at the conclusion of a dream. At that time, she was just over fourteen years old and was living with her aunt since she was angry with her mother. Toward her aunt, and especially toward her older male cousin, she felt great embarrassment (as she had felt toward her mother in the dream).

I pointed out to her the temporal proximity, not coincidental, of the previously mentioned beating scene and this bed-wetting incident. I expressed my suspicion that she could have recalled these two incidents so well since they were her very last memories of this type.

I requested that she try to recall earlier cases of bed-wetting and stated that it was highly unlikely for this to have occurred only once in her case.

Without being able directly to deny such earlier occasions, she was able to recall only this one incident with certainty. Yet from isolated and noticeable details of the dream content, one gains the convincing impression that such coprophilic[42] and urophilic tendencies, later well repressed and completely superseded, were highly significant in the young woman's childhood.

They were significant not only as a source of autoerotic pleasure, and to a certain extent also as "object love" in related play activities with her friends, but also as one type of activity forbidden by her mother, punishment for which helped to intensify the young woman's inimical feelings toward her.

This first, pre-historical period of infantile eroticism can be reconstructed from the following dream elements.

In her description of the summer experiences in her hometown reflected in the dream, one unassuming detail seems noticeable since it stands in contradiction to the otherwise rather accurate replication of reality.

The young woman, who is pedantically concerned with cleanliness, had been surprised by a passing rain on one of her first walks in her new white dress. The rain, as she was pleased to discover, produced no traces of mud. In the dream content, this detail appears precisely as its opposite: the ground suddenly becomes muddy although it has not rained.

Behind this noticeable inversion of reality, we may suspect that an especially intensive repression is at work, also suggested by the surprise expressly emphasised by the dreamer in the dream content. She now stated that at the start of the rain, she held her dress rather high in order to protect it as she went forward,[43] continually fearing that she could be seen by someone (as with tearing off the ears of grain in the dream).

I suppose that behind this lifting of her skirts in this area free of other persons, where one would not like to be seen, there lies a hint at urination (rain[24]), while excrement is already clearly expressed in the German word *Kot* ("excrement" or "mud"). I can support this interpretation with another detail that was subsequently provided, where this bodily function is clearly indicated. The young woman's unembarrassed "squatting by the gate of the house," while acting as if she were busy with something else, reveals with infantile naiveté the meaning of lifting the skirts.

Here, the fear of being observed seems to be an expression of the repression of the child's exhibitionism and lack of embarrassment. This exhibitionism also reveals itself in a symbolic hint belonging to the excrement complex—a hint allowing us to suspect that our dreamer, as an enthusiastic playmate and observer of the bodily functions of her age cohorts, repeatedly saw their genitals.

In describing the second dream, the dreamer commented: "Through the gate, which stood open, I saw her garden, which attracted me very much." This element is analogous to an almost identically worded subsequent description from the first dream. ["*Through this gate-like opening I saw a garden and thought: 'God, if only I could go into that garden'— but I didn't go in.*"] It utilises the ancient sexual-symbolic meaning of the garden,[26] which is identical to that of the gate (Latin *porta*). Also, the black substance that is left unidentified ("plum jam, or something similar") which the young woman who was squatting held in her hand, should be interpreted as referring to excrement, and stirring around in the mud with a stick (or brush) refers back to infantile play with faeces.

This young woman is apparently a personification of the dreamer herself in childhood. Furthermore, the dream itself, in its own manner of expression, which is sometimes to be taken quite literally, suggests the identification of rain with urine and of mud with excrement.

When the ground suddenly becomes "muddy" without there having been rain, only the process of excretion can be intended. If there were any doubts as to the correctness of these connections, they are diffused by the embarrassed efforts of the dreamer to delete her own subsequent comments, discussed above, from the written account of the dream when those comments came up in the discussion.

She averred that one could not allow such things to remain in the written account, that this would be completely inappropriate, and so on. In brief, she acted precisely as if she had already accepted my interpretation before it was even presented to her, and was therefore now demonstrating the connected affect of embarrassment.

This affect reveals all too clearly its origins in the complex of uncleanliness. From the complex of housebreaking pets, an inconspicuous comment about the second dream becomes enlightening for our understanding of the little girls' play.

In the account of the dream, the young woman holding something black in her hand also had a dog beside her, a hint that can be interpreted as a coprophilic and urophilic characterisation of this entire scenario from early childhood.

As a child, the dreamer herself had been engaged in the housebreaking of cats; indeed, she had applied the same method she feared her mother would use in her own case.[25]

With the identification of this early infantile anal and urethral eroticism as the deepest unconscious dream material, I would have exhausted the entire dream content—from conscious connections while awake, and through the wealth of preconscious fantasy life, to the unknown sources—if a still unexplained and disregarded detail did not point to a further decisive unconscious source. The unusually ambiguous emphasis on an incestuous perspective has allowed me to recognise powerful processes of repression, which found expression in far-reaching and multiple distortions of the greeting scene.

It lies in the nature of analytic work that in detecting these processes I had to manage without the assistance of the dreamer. Nor could I, in the context of this detail, rely on my skills of interpretation without being accused of arbitrariness.

Indeed, Freud has warned against making major conclusions—such as a tendency to homosexuality (women, women's rooms)—based on just one detail that could be interpreted in a sexual-symbolic way. I might have been satisfied to end the nearly completed interpretation of the first dream by mentioning the probability of such a deeply hidden homosexual current. Yet precisely at this decisive point, the initially emphasised, unusual character of the dream comes to my aid, very clearly revealing this suspected but ultimate meaning of the dream, which could otherwise not be proven with certainty. Here, I am thinking especially of the detail at the end of the second dream, whose characteristic relationship to the first dream will justify both the presentation of this analysis and its title.

Only now am I truly faced with the task of acknowledging and evaluating this peculiar detail of the dream. Here, I am led by an idea supported by the unique parallelism of the two dreams, and with whose help the unconscious meaning of the greeting ceremony can be revealed—the meaning foremost in the last portion of my interpretive work.

To verify my suspicion, I asked the dreamer to tell me her physical position at the end of the dream. She initially avoided providing a detailed description of this sexual (orgasmic) situation by pointing out that she was "lying in exactly the same way as in the first dream—before the queen."[27] This information, which I expected, tells me more than a detailed description of the final scene could ever tell me.

Indeed, it demonstrates that the unusual leave-taking ceremony formally represents nothing but the sexual gratification achieved, in the absence of the mother, at the end of the second dream. When the strict mother is present, this (homosexual) gratification is, as it were, forbidden and inhibited. Thus, in reference to this point, I also recognise that the two dreams stand in a characteristic mutual opposition.

In the first dream, the mother is presented as a disturber—as an obstacle to sexual pleasure—while in the second dream, through the elimination of this sexual inhibition, the forbidden can be done with impunity. The first dream shows the mother not only as an obstacle to homosexual pleasure, but as an obstacle to childhood eroticism in all forms.

As a competitor for the love of the father, she stands disturbingly in the way (departure of the king and queen), mercilessly punishes persistent pleasurable bed-wetting, prevents through her strict surveillance all masturbatory gratification (opening of the forbidden door), puts a stop to erotic relationships with female friends (rooms),[4] and watches over her daughter's interactions with young men (tutor).[19]

In the second dream, however, where the mother has been eliminated, one can "tear off ears of grain" with impunity and experience pleasure with one's female friends uninhibited; one can indulge one's coprophilic and urophilic tendencies. In brief, one can engage in infantile sexual activities.

Here, I notice that in the first dream, which takes place far from the dreamer's home and to some extent involves fantasies of the future, the mother is present, while in the second dream, which takes place in the dreamer's hometown, the mother is absent.[5]

Now I know that the absence of the mother represents the condition for the sexual freedom of the daughter, which the dreamer sought to obtain, in a reversal of the dream wish, by travelling away from her hometown. In the dream, though, she wishes to be back in her hometown and in her childhood so as to escape the inner restrictions and calamities of her current life.

The dream presents these in an improved edition, as it were—free from the disturbing influence of the mother, just as the dreamer wished as a child: the mother should travel away (departure/death complex), and the dreamer herself should be able to remain at home (i.e. with the father) in undisturbed freedom.

Temporarily disregarding the unavoidable wish corrections, the first dream, clothed in the form of an accusation and a reproach, depicts the dreamer's life as it would have to develop under the inhibiting and disturbing influence of her mother.

Yet the second dream, naturally also in the form of reactivated infantile wish-fulfilment, shows how her life would have developed if her mother had not been there, that is, if she had died (corresponding to the dreamer's unconscious wish).

The close of the first dream, which ends with the departure (death) of the mother, is thus the essential condition for the second dream, which brings the longed-for sexual gratification.

Freud has pointed out that dreams make use of such a double depiction as an indication of causal relationships,[29] and has discussed this insight in the context of the dream of a patient; the dream depicts the departure fantasy, also indirectly indicated in our case (Rank, 1909, p. 65 ff.). "The thought concealed behind the one dream can be expressed as: 'Because I come from this home, from these petty and unappealing circumstances …' The main dream takes up the same thought and portrays it transformed by wish fulfilment: 'I am of noble descent.' This actually signifies: 'Due to my lowly origins, the course of my life was as it was'" (Freud, 1909a, p. 230).

We could say that underlying our case is the grammatical relationship between a conditional clause and a desiderative clause [expressing the wishes of the subject of the clause (Translator's Note)]. "Because of my mother, I was unable to achieve sexual fulfilment in any form (thus including social life and marriage) (first dream). But if she had died, I would have been able to do everything with impunity and achieve everything unhindered (second dream). But now she is living. If only things were reversed (from their real state) as in the second dream!"

Beyond this reversal for the depiction of the wish (utinam, "if only")—a wish the dream can only express positively (in a reversal of the undesired reality)—the reversed relationship in this multiply complicated and still relatively transparent dream maintains a deeper meaning. This again brings me closer to the final, yet-to-be-revealed, sense of the greeting scene.

At the Vienna Psychoanalytic Society, Professor Freud has on occasion pointed out that dreams in which something is reversed or can be reversed generally have a homosexual meaning. These dreams are not to be confused with those in whose interpretation a detail can be taken in the opposite sense.

Rather, these disguised homosexual dreams usually contain in their manifest text a hint about their "reversal." In the content of our second dream, the dreamer is surprised that the barley is ripe first, and then the rye—though it is usually the reverse. This clear hint in the manifest dream text reveals, on the one hand, that there is indeed something in this dream that should be interpreted in reverse, but, on the other hand, the dream confirms the empirical rule of dream interpretation, mentioned above, since it is really beginning to reveal itself as a homosexual dream.

Thus, as a justification for the fact that in the greeting scene all the elements appear as their opposite, I note that in the orgasmic situation analogous to the greeting scene, the dreamer herself feels and acts in a reversed (inverted) manner.

To uncover the further and presumably deeper connections between these two dream scenes, I require further information about the events and persons of the final situation leading to the orgasmic act. The investigation of this final situation is the most delicate portion of my analytical task, yet it promises me the deepest meaning and final solution to the dream.

Thus, telling her that a complete interpretation would otherwise be impossible, I attempted to extract from the dreamer an unembarrassed and maximally accurate depiction of the final scene and a closer characterisation of the two young women appearing there. This produced the following material, entirely sufficient for the suspected final interpretation; below, this material will be presented in the words of the dreamer herself, without reference to the technical and mental difficulties in obtaining it.

> The first friend in the dream (A.) has the same name as my younger sister. All I know about her is that she had a child out of wedlock. The second friend (B.) is called Franzi; she was also in my class at school.

I remember her especially well because she was already so fully developed and mature (excessively mature, mature early) when she was thirteen that she was no longer permitted to attend school. We girls used to refer to her as "the mother," and she really was like a mother in her physical relation and behaviour toward us. I only associated with her because of her wealthy parents, who had a large garden and bought her many expensive playthings. I was actually angry with her, as in the dream.

Due to her special physical development, she began associating with young men at an early age, and so my mother forbade me to associate with her. She has an older sister, Rosa, who is already married now.

Later, our dreamer also recalled another friend with the same name, who had also associated with young men at an early age.[10a] As in the first case, our dreamer associated with her mainly due to her parents' wealth, and not so much because of any inclination toward her.

All these real-life memories made me curious as to whether something similar to the final scene of the second dream had actually occurred with Franzi. Though this suspicion, so close at hand, was not confirmed, it turned out that at the age of ten our dreamer was in the habit of playing "father and mother" in this way with another female friend, K.

Understandably, her conscious recollection of masturbation also dates from this same period. Yet it is extremely important to note that this playing "father and mother" had already begun earlier with her brother, whose name is also Franzi.

Here, I seem to have reached a certain stopping point, and I shall interrupt the investigation so as to test this material for its interpretive value. Although this material does not confirm specific results of the analysis thus far (e.g. the significance of the masturbation complex), nor make other details immediately comprehensible, it does provide a new insight decisive for the further resolution of the dream. Indeed, since the homosexual act proves to be a recapitulation of real infantile experiences of gratification, the question arises as to why the real sexual partner is not also recapitulated. Rather, an apparently indifferent person appears in her stead.

Now, on the basis of the material discussed above, the answer lies at hand. The sexual partner in the dream is first of all a substitute for the mother, towards whom, apparently, the girl's homosexual affection was principally directed ("She really was like a mother"). [*The dreamer's embarrassment in the presence of her mother (of the same gender) also clearly indicates a repressed homosexual affection.*]

I might, with psychiatric indignation, reject such a feeling as disgusting, but before doing so, it would be good to understand the origin of such feelings. Freud (1910a) has shown that many perversions are merely the pleasurable manipulation of the sexual organs from earliest childhood carried forth with the sexual energy of the adult.

This homosexual state of being in love with the mother we will only be able to understand, for the time being, as an intensification of the normal affection of the child. This affection has its origin in the act of nursing at the mother's breast, and those familiar with the psychology of the dream will hardly find it too bold to suppose this infantile situation as the deepest essence of the homosexual dream scene.

After some intense questioning, the dreamer provided new information fully confirming this supposition. She indicated that in the dream she had lain on her friend while holding the young woman's breasts in her hands and kissing them, which fully corresponds to the position of the child nursing at the mother's breast.

Thus, the deepest unconscious dream wish aims for the re-establishment of this infantile situation, which the dreamer places back into the time when the social and erotic calamities of her present life did not exist—into the blissful time when there were no worries about the supply of food[5] and no lovesickness, when hunger and love found complete gratification to the greatest degree and in one single act.[5a]

But contrasting again with this conception, you might object by asking why this innocent wish tendency did not find direct expression in the dream, instead being hidden behind a similar but more offensive situation. Now it is clear that the dreamer would not wish herself back in the situation of a nursing baby, but wants only to express her regret that she no longer has access to such complete and uninhibited gratification as she once enjoyed at her mother's breast. In other words, in her unconscious fantasy she has sexualised these infantile acts—a process Freud has revealed as typical in the later reprocessing of childhood fantasies (1909c, p. 393).

This apparent contradiction is resolved by our knowledge of the processes of repression: such an exaggerated effect of hatred toward a person one is close to can be explained as the result of the repression of an originally very intense loving inclination toward that person.

The dreamer was not able consciously to recall such an excessively tender relationship with her mother. However, she reported that this had indeed been true of her sister, a few years younger than she,[36] whom she had repeatedly ridiculed due to her tender attachment to their mother.

Even during her last visit in the summer, she had not been able to refrain from ridiculing her sister about this, but was corrected by her mother with the comment that as a child she had been even more tender and affectionate than her sister. This she denied most emphatically, even to her mother. Naturally! She had repressed this loving inclination only too well. The mother herself was not placed in the homosexual dream situation because the dreamer certainly feels no love for her now.

But the mother character of the female friend and the situation of the dreamer who, as it were, nurses at her breast, shows without a doubt that this homosexual inclination applied originally to the mother and had been awakened through her.

Simultaneously, in the greeting scene, the dream expresses disappointment and regret that this tender relationship with the mother so soon dimmed, being inverted (reversed) to the opposite. Only now do we understand why the dreamer lies before the punishing mother in the first dream, and not, as in the second dream (as a child), upon the loving mother.[27]

She reproaches her mother for having, through her coldness and strictness, driven the tender (homosexual) affection out of her, as it were, so that she was obliged to satisfy her need for affection through other objects. If we concentrate in more detail on the dreamer's sexual partner, the dream will again reveal the nature of these objects.

This sexual partner is taken up into the dream content not only because of the "motherly" constitution of her body, but also because of the identity of her name to that of the dreamer's brother. Thus, she is an object condensed from various ideals, just as artists often condense several objects into one. She has the body and being of the dreamer's mother, the name of her brother, and the facial features of her female friend.

If we also consider the dreamer's statement that her friend has a robust and somewhat masculine build and shows her masculine aspect, especially in her voice,[38] it becomes clear that the dreamer's sexual object is androgynous, bisexual, and we easily recognise that this results from the bisexual orientation of the dreamer herself, who, in the orgasm scene, acts in a thoroughly masculine way.[23a]

As mentioned above, lying on the mother's breast is not reproduced in the dream in the innocent manner of a nursing child, but is transformed into a masculine coital fantasy involving the mother.

Nor is it difficult to determine the origin of the material in this fantasy: it apparently derives from an identification with the father, whose role the dreamer wishes to play with respect to her mother.

She now admitted that in playing "father and mother," she had always been the boy (the "father"), and that as a girl she had always shown a boyish character and tendencies; she was often told by her mother that she should have been a boy.

She also mentioned frankly that she had always wished she were a man, and still does. When I asked her why, she responded: "Well, because of the girls."[39] Since childhood, she has also felt the desire to dress as a man,[40] and she remembers two times when this actually occurred. Once when she was fifteen, soon after the death of her father, she put on the cadet uniform of a female classmate's brother.

In this attire, she walked through the streets smoking cigarettes, with her classmate as her "sweetheart" on her arm—to the surprise of the onlookers, who had never before seen this "smartly dressed cadet."

On another occasion, when she was about twenty, she had put on her cousin's cap and uniform. She was noticed by a woman with whom she was on friendly terms, who told her: "You will never be a bride." She had responded with surprise: "But why?" and was told: "Because you've put on men's clothing. Don't you know the traditional belief about that?"

This prediction made a big impression on the young woman, and even now, when describing this conversation, she commented that the woman might turn out to be right. She also casually mentioned that she felt no strong desire to be married, and would only marry to ensure her own welfare.[16]

Analysis reveals the deepest foundation of this feeling. As the deepest meaning of the dream, it reveals the wish: "If things were only reversed! If only I were a man instead of a woman!" The dream sequence shows her this wish fulfilled, for she behaves—at least at the end of the second dream—in a thoroughly masculine way.

The dreamer's comment that she had lain on her female friend in the same position as when she had lain on the floor before the queen in the first dream reveals the formal identity of the greeting ceremony and the homosexual scene of orgasm.

Since my analysis of that scene reveals the dreamer's bisexual feelings as a basic feature of the second dream, I can now seek in the contents of the first dream a hidden tendency for bisexual wish-fulfilment.

In this endeavour, in which I shall perhaps go beyond the framework of my current task, I will have to rely on clues that are few and not always secure, for it is precisely the homosexual orientation which has, in the first dream, undergone the most extensive distortions and disguises. This is the layer of feelings where interpretation cannot be completely carried forward to its culmination—where the dream, as it were, flows back into the deepest levels of the unconscious.

But from the elucidation of the second dream, I can be certain about the long-suspected symbolic sense of the rooms, which in the first dream occur in a fully masculine sense (women's rooms).

For in the second dream, the dreamer feels and acts like a man. Here, in apparent contrast with the facts, the symbolism is shown to be a secure psychological criterion applying even to the difference between the sexes.

Here, though, I also recognise that the dreamer's reaction to the interpretation equating the rooms with women—which she had rejected with the comment: "As far as I'm concerned, they may be images of men"—is not only an unconscious "yes," but the mental acknowledgement of her bisexual orientation.

According to her dream thoughts, it doesn't matter whether they are women's rooms or men's rooms. Yet her stronger, unconscious inclination, as the dream reveals, is for women. Therefore, in reality, she did not accept the fiancé favoured by her mother as a match for her.

In the dream, he does not even come close to her; she flees from him to her infantile sexual activities (bed-wetting, "breaking off ears of grain," female friends).

She therefore also avoids her childhood friend Z., who she fears will "address" her (i.e. invite her to a hotel). In this context, the words of the king are also to be understood as a rejection of the female role in sexual intercourse. He says to her: "Pardon, this is not your room." Likewise, the fact that the tutor is prevented from reaching her in the room expresses not only a punishment by the mother, but also the wish to have nothing to do with the man while she is in the forbidden room.

Only the identification with the chambermaid finally reveals the beginning of a truly female coital fantasy ("The chambermaid had to pack her master's things quickly"). This fantasy, though, is not carried forth to its culmination ("Whether they went away, I don't know"). Nor is it an ideal feminine fantasy ("I didn't see the child again"). On the deepest level, it expresses her wish that she not marry and that she have no children.

In this sense, the child appearing at the beginning of the first dream, whom I was able to interpret as an infantile image of the dreamer herself, actually reveals in just a few words the deepest sense of the entire dream sequence and of the destiny of the dreamer.

Indeed, she says of the child: "I don't know whether it was a boy or a girl." Given the content of the unconscious dream thoughts, the dreamer would be well justified in stating this about herself.

The first dream is mainly negative, and demonstrates the rejection of the dreamer's femininity, yet in isolated features, it already suggests the male position that breaks through openly in the second dream.

It is expressed in an especially characteristic way in the tutor scene in the first dream, thus far inadequately explained. Given the interpretation thus far, I must conceive it as a representation of the masculine feelings of the dreamer.[34]

A tutor is the male complement of a governess (images of a man versus a woman). In the dream, the identification of these two persons is indicated by the fact that they do exactly the same thing.

Like the governess, the tutor must "likewise" take his leave from the queen, and like her, he "also" receives permission to visit the room.

Disregarding the interpretive possibilities discussed above (supervision by the mother, hotel fantasy with rejection of coitus), the fact that he is admitted to the room only after some difficulty is connected with the peculiar character and structure of the dream sequence.

The first dream shows the obstruction of all attempts at sexual gratification, achieved only in the second dream. Indeed, I notice here that
the tutor's attempt to enter the forbidden room, just like the greeting
ceremony earlier, represents nothing but the obstruction of sexual gratification, and expresses the dreamer's regret that she is unable to carry
out her masculine role with a woman (women's rooms).

I begin to suspect that all the other situations of the first dream represent the same thing. Just as entrance to the room is made difficult for
the tutor, the dreamer is unable to enter the enticing garden that attracts
her so much in the first dream.

This wish to penetrate the garden, too, is a masculine fantasy. Disregarding the aggressive role taken on by the dreamer in this context,
the garden, as already mentioned, is an ancient and universally known
symbol of the female genitals.

Likewise, the subsequent dream situation in which the dreamer unin-
tentionally enters the king's washroom rather than her own is another
unsuccessful attempt at achieving the longed-for sexual gratification.

This scene, incidentally, is connected by one detail with the act of
orgasm, and also represents its obstruction. The dreamer commented
that the day before the dream, she had seen the brother of the young
boy who had received the siskin brushing up his wet hair just as the
king had done in the dream. ["*He was brushing his hair up; it was still
wet and standing on end.*"]

This boy, about fifteen years old, whose name was also Franzi, was
somewhat in love with the dreamer, and she also showed some affection
for him. She had noticed how he wet his hair and carefully brushed it
up before going to school; she remarked that it seemed ridiculous to her
that a young man could be as vain as a young woman.

Here again, we find a bisexual reference, and will relate the dreamer's affection for the young man to the fact that at that age he lacked a
strongly masculine appearance and more strongly resembled a young
woman.

We must also recall that Franzi is the nickname both for the masculine name (Franz) and for the feminine name (Franziska). A scene
from two years earlier also occurred to the dreamer in which another
of her half-grown protégés, also in love with her, was also brushing his
hair before a mirror. He then asked whether he was now handsome and

whether she found him attractive.[37] His name was Poldi, a nickname commonly used for the masculine name (Leopold) as well as for the feminine name (Leopoldine). Also with this young man, the dreamer emphasised the trait of vanity.

Thus, the king in the dream personifies not only the dreamer's father and her fiancé, but also her brother, and, given the identity in name, the young man—bisexual (female) as it were—representing the brother.

Indeed, with her brother, just as with her female friend, she had really played "father and mother," always taking on the masculine role. Her unintended entry into the pink room is thus a renewed attempt to achieve masculine gratification (on her brother), which is, however, rejected with a reference to her female gender ("This is not your room").[14]

I have just discussed as well the fact that the final dream situation too (when the king travels away) represents the obstruction of the pursuit of gratification—this time heterosexual. Yet this coital fantasy remains vague and incomplete since it relates in the unconscious to the father (king), with whom of course she hoped to remain alone after the departure (death) of the queen (mother).

In the first dream, the four relevant situations are the greeting ceremony, the tutor's wish to penetrate the lilac room (and the dreamer's similar desire to enter the garden), the unintended entry into the pink room, and the scene of the king's departure (in the reception room).

I recognise all four situations as obstructed and unsuccessful attempts to achieve one of the longed-for types of sexual gratifications actually gained in the second dream. Thus it will not seem too bold if, as a sort of experimental proof of this interpretation, I adduce the dreamer's admission that the four dashes at the end of her written account of the second dream signify four repetitions of the sex act and of the pleasurable feelings. This would explain in a completely sufficient manner the four unsuccessful attempts at gratification in the first dream.[37a]

In the orgasm scene at the close of the second dream, the dreamer acts as a male (bisexual), but in the first dream she leaves neither the homosexual nor the heterosexual modes of gratification untried. And just as the sexual object in the orgasm scene is bisexual, the objects in the first dream are bisexual as well.

Throughout the entire dream sequence, the dreamer herself in all her personifications, and all of her sexual objects, are bisexual beings—not only the tutor and his complement, the governess, not only Franzi and Poldi, but also the little child, of whom it is not known whether it is a boy or a girl.

A sexual-symbolic key reveals that the lilac room, later described in detail as decorated with Chinese furnishings, also has a bisexual sense beyond the urophilic sense discussed above.

In the hotel fantasy, the lilac room shows the dreamer as a woman, but in the tutor situation, it shows her as a man. Stekel has pointed out that, in his experience, the Chinese are a frequently encountered symbol of bisexuality, probably due to the *queue* [a braid of hair behind the head, worn by Chinese men in Qing Dynasty China (Translator's Note)]. Since the analysis thus far has established the dreamer's bisexual orientation beyond all doubt, I can accept for the current dream as well this sexual-symbolic meaning of all things "Chinese."

Thus, I immediately understand the meaning of the dream thought: "I must prostrate myself like a Chinese person (like a bisexual being)," and I understand the marriage fantasy that turns away from the conventional objects and turns instead to a distinguished Chinese (man–woman).[16] Finally, I understand also the Chinese garments of the queen-mother, who, as a sexual object, is perceived as bisexual (Franzi).[28]

Correspondingly, the first dream image shows the mother as a Chinese woman or room, and in terms of content, the penetration of the (male) dreamer into this forbidden room, as tutor, is the direct anticipation of the orgasmic act in which of course the dreamer achieves coitus with her mother, while the greeting scene prepares the orgasm in a merely formal way (position). Yet given the manner of the attempt at gratification (prone position), the greeting scene also belongs to the masturbation complex.

Only now do I notice that the four attempts at gratification in the first dream correspond to four forms of experienced or fantasised gratification.

First, the dreamer attempts to achieve gratification through masturbation (prone position). Then, she attempts it by taking on the male role with the mother (penetration into the lilac room). Then (in the pink room), she attempts it with her brother through a recreation of playing "father and mother." Then, at the end of the first dream, she attempts it with a female love fantasy relating to her father (king).

It is characteristic of the condensation work of the dream that to trigger the gratification of orgasm a situation is chosen that provides all the possibilities for gratification sought in vain in the first dream. Masturbatory gratification in the prone position is expressed especially strongly.[47] Indeed, the entire act is only a "masturbation" carried out on an object, like playing "father and mother."

In addition, the orgasmic situation also provides room for the male fantasy of achieving gratification with the mother (lilac room) through identification with the father (incest fantasy). It also provides room for the repetition of the pleasurable (sadistic) act of wrestling with her brother.

One could argue against the claim that the first dream deals with wish-fulfilment by arguing that it mainly depicts dissatisfaction, sexual inhibition, and demeaning acts of punishment. To refute such an argument, I need only refer to the second dream, which offers the dreamer the most complete sexual gratification, and to the close relation and unitary characters of the two dreams.

The act of punishment in the first dream especially contradicts any wish-fulfilment. Yet it becomes comprehensible from the dreamer's multiply over-determined guilty conscience, and in other ways. It could not have established itself in such an undisguised manner if it did not express an especially deep wish-fulfilment, as we shall demonstrate.

But before I discuss this last root of the dream, a root which permeates the entire drive life of the dreamer, there is still a significant infantile source that must be mentioned in addition to the previously noted current preconscious and unconscious conditions of the dreamer's sense of guilt.

This infantile source establishes a connection, previously left open, between the beating scene experienced in reality and the beating scene as reproduced in the dream.

As one of the basic sources of the unconscious sense of guilt conditioning the sexual inhibition noted in the first dream, I have identified the fear that an offence in the sphere of the erotic will be discovered. In the real beating scene, recalled as a punishment in the dream, the dreamer was punished for lying about a visit with a female friend—a visit she had wished to keep a secret.

Here, a connection was missing which becomes clear only through analysis of the second dream. The dreamer had really been angry with her friend Franzi, and this is suggested in the dream itself by a detail which openly contradicts the content of the final scene.

It is still not fully clear why, at the end of the dream, the dreamer so lovingly takes her friend, with whom she even claims to be angry in the dream, as a sexual object. Indeed, this was never the case in reality. But I have recognised that this contradictory role is due to her identification with her mother, a connection which now becomes fully meaningful by considering a new side of the dream thoughts.

I know that the dreamer had been angry with her mother for a long time, just as she had been with her real sexual partner K., as she later revealed. In this anger complex, I have found the knot that ties together the three persons as the combined sexual object in the dream.

The deeper sense of this connection and its relationship to the sense of guilt become clear from the young woman's comment that whenever she was angry with her friend K., she constantly feared that her friend would reveal her sexual secret to her mother—playing "father and mother" with K.

She further commented that she always comforted herself with the thought that her friend would not reveal the secret due to her own involvement in the offence. The dreamer does not recall a punishment for any erotic transgression (including bed-wetting); such a recollection could serve as a direct confirmation of our assumption of a sexual source for the sense of guilt. Yet her comment that she always feared the discovery and subsequent punishment of a wholly sexual offence can be taken as a fully sufficient proof.

Now I understand the awakening and the inhibiting influence of the infantile sense of guilt, which receives input from various levels of psychological life. The dreamer's current guilty conscience, which, due to her inappropriate departure from her mother fears *Krampus's* threatening switch (rather than expecting the hoped-for gift), is intensified by the preconscious sense of guilt associated with the remembered beating scene when the dreamer was fourteen years old (the lie about K.).

Also intensified is the unconscious sense of guilt of infantile origin, which after every forbidden instance of sexual gratification expects discovery due to the angry friend and punishment by the "evil" mother.

As I have already suggested, however, it would be too one-sided to see in the beating scene in the dream only the act of punishment, reproduced by the multiply determined sense of guilt. Freud (1907, p. 81) has on occasion explained that in the case of a person with such a predisposition, such dreams are to be regarded as masochistic wish-fulfilments.

Indeed, the greeting scene, which I was compelled to interpret as an attempted sex act, also gives the impression of a masochistic beating.[42a] As for the dreamer herself, the most prominent character trait that will be noticed by an unbiased observer is her proud, domineering, and strong-willed masculine-active personality.

Indeed, this fully accords with her psychosexual constitution as uncovered in the course of interpretive work. Yet in becoming more familiar with the emotional life of the dreamer, it becomes clear that at certain times, completely in contrast with her current personality, she can exhibit a sentimental, soft, and maudlin disposition.

This apparent contradiction becomes comprehensible through the insight that both sadistic and masochistic drive impulses and character traits are regularly encountered in one and the same individual (Freud, 1910a, p. 19; Rank, 1907, p. 31).

These are usually distributed such that one of the two drive directions is almost completely repressed, and, through the unconscious, is utilised to strengthen or partially paralyse the other, dominant component.

Yet the nearly simultaneous coexistence and alternation of the two opposite emotional currents has a neurotic element, for which we would claim that the intensive processes of repression in our dreamer (cf. the parent complex) are responsible.

When asked about the noticeable coexistence of these two contrasting sides of her personality, the young woman was able, among various insignificant details, to report on an "oddity" in her developmental years.

She said that as a child she had greatly enjoyed slaughtering fowl, especially chickens. She had always actively asked to do this under the pretence that she would need to learn this skill if she wished to become an efficient housewife in the future. Once, however, she did not succeed in fully severing the chicken's head (cf. cutting off the ears of grain and seeing the chickens eat them, Endnote 5). The bird broke free and ran around the yard, half slaughtered. She was extremely scared, and feared the bird would attack her. Since that time, she could not kill an animal—not at any price. On being asked, she said that at the time of this incident she was about fourteen years old.[45]

Today, the young woman, especially toward animals, is compassionate and gentle in exaggerated measure, yet in a manner characteristic of her drive life: she said repeatedly that she loved this or that animal so much that she would like best of all to crush it or strangle it, as she had often done in childhood with doves, which of course were not among the fowl to be slaughtered.

As noted, the day before the dream, she had hugged and kissed the siskin. This episode served as a trigger for the dream; along with the chicken scene in the second dream, reminding us of her cruelty as a child, it shows clearly what an essential part these components of her drive life and character play in the origin and structure of the dream.

Indeed, this is true in its active (sadistic) as well as its passive (masochistic) manifestations. Here, too, the two portions of the dream stand in the characteristic opposition I have previously emphasised several times: the first dream exhibits mainly masochistic traits.

This is true not only in the crudely physical sense (beating scene), but also in the general inhibition of the dreamer's aggressive sexual nature, and not least in a psychological sense (submission, etc.).

The second dream, by contrast, provides the active counterpart to the first dream: the grasping masculinity (tearing off ears of grain), the stubborn defiance (cf. Endnote 5), and the aggressive, masculine sexual role in the gratification situation.

But already in the first dream—in the way the submission is made ironic, in the breaking free from sexual inhibition (the tutor does penetrate into the room), and in the attempt to escape the beating (cf. Endnote 5 and Endnote 25)—the dreamer's rebellious, sadistically defiant underlying personality shines through.

And finally, of course, in the identification with the mother, also suggested in the dream, her fully sadistic orientation of drives breaks through, for in this role, the dreamer herself is the active one carrying out the beating.[46]

On the other hand, her sadistic wishes for the punishment and death of her mother must have been augmented by the embarrassing chastisements administered by her mother, which she experienced with shame.

Thus, as the basic character of the entire dream sequence, there is an inner ambiguity of feeling entirely corresponding to the exterior division into two parts. This ambiguity of feeling permeates the dreamer's entire life of drives, feelings, and thoughts. [*The young woman would definitely belong to the personality type described in Freud, 1909c, which would also correspond to her strengthened sadistic orientation of drives. It is presumably this basic personality and its retention that have enabled her thus far to escape hysteria.*]

Through a characteristic division into two complementary components, the dream sequence expresses the fusion of the opposing pairs sadism versus masochism, and male versus female.

It gives expression as well to several unresolved alternatives retained from the infantile constellation: death of the father versus death of the mother, love for the mother versus hatred toward her, and finally a more superficial relation, reward versus punishment by the mother, the point where the dream work begins.

Theoretical observations

Finally, in providing a summary of the theoretical discussion of the dream and of its now complete analysis, I will need to be brief: the interpretation itself has already occupied me extensively and has taken up a significant amount of space.

Most importantly, I wish to summarise the proof of the reliability of Freud's technique and theory of dream interpretation, a proof that has been developed in detail during the entire course of my interpretive work.

At no point was it necessary to go beyond the bounds of Freud's approach to arrive at a satisfactory explanation of the dream content, which at first appeared to make no sense, and to reach a sufficient understanding of the mental mechanisms and factors of dream life involved in its structure.

Yet if isolated insights are especially emphasised in the following discussion, this is justified by the fact that, on the one hand, the basic tenets of dream theory are still appreciated far too little, given their theoretical and practical significance; it has not often enough been possible to explain and reconfirm them through examples. On the other hand, such an emphasis may allow us to grasp more clearly certain theoretical insights only hinted at in *The Interpretation of Dreams*.

To the reader accustomed to approaching every such investigation with a critical bias, some aspects of the preceding dream interpretation may seem arbitrary, forced, or insufficiently solid.

Yet even the most biased sceptics, unless they are completely blind, will be unable to escape the impression that dreams, far from constituting the meaningless play of our unoccupied nerves, can not only gain a possible meaning through artful interpretation, but can even reveal, through insights into their innermost structure, the deepest sense of the individual psychological and human life under investigation.

Indeed, we see that the entire mind in its broadest scope, with all its current and infantile complexes, is somehow involved, directly or indirectly, in the formation of dreams. Thus, this confirms Freud's strongly emphasised finding, based on experience, that the "dream is only seldom the representation, or, one could say, the dramatic portrayal of a single thought. Rather, it portrays an entire series of thoughts, a web of thoughts" (Freud, 1907). "The dream is regularly ambiguous. Not only can several wish fulfilments be united within it, side by side, but one sense, one wish fulfilment, can cover another until, at the deepest level, one arrives at the fulfilment of a wish from earliest childhood" (Freud, 1900, p. 1).

Of all these meanings, though, the most important one, the one actually active in the formation of dreams and which one must designate as the actual sense of the dream, lies hidden and anchored in the depths of the unconscious.

Without exception, this sense relates to an infantile sexual wish (drive), long repressed, which then, connecting itself with a current sexual wish (with an erotic need in the broadest sense), again attempts to find gratification, in disguised form, in the dream.

Regularly, then, against the background of repressed infantile sexual material and aided by that material, the dream presents current, generally also erotic wishes as fulfilled—in a disguised and symbolically clothed form.[50] [*This expansion and specialisation of the Freudian formula (1900, p. 115) is only undertaken based on additions to the second edition (1909a, especially p. 197), which are to be interpreted in this sense, and on personal communications by Freud.*]

Current erotic dissatisfaction in the broadest (also mental) sense flees back, as it were, to the blissful time of childhood ("regression" of the libido), when there were neither external nor internal sexual inhibitions, and when erotic gratification of the need for affection, given the innocence of such gratification, could be effected completely and without inhibition.

These "wish impulses from childhood, indestructible and not subject to inhibition" (Freud, 1900, p. 375), have now, in the course of development, lost their naïve innocence; they are rejected by the conscious thoughts of the adult (1900, p. 375, "Repression").

Therefore, the infantile situation of gratification cannot be presented in undisguised form in the dream content because an obvious "fulfilment of these wishes would no longer produce a pleasurable affect, but an unpleasurable one" (1900, p. 375). Thus, we must consider the disguising of dreams (distortion) to be the work of sexual inhibitions established since childhood (cf. Freud, 1910a). A consequence of these normal processes of repression is the development of layers in mental life, discussed by Freud in the section "Psychology of Dream Processes" (1900).

Due to its unique structure, the dream I have presented makes this layering truly tangible. This layering and its regressive course (Freud) in the formation of dreams helps to explain why our first dream, linked to recent events of the day, mainly presents fantasies of the future (current daydreams) in an apparently asexual, sublimated form, while the second dream, with deeper sources, presents the historical and prehistorical foundations of the "mythically" embellished prior dream, as well as current and infantile sexual gratification, in a rather undisguised form.[48]

In this light, only the first dream can actually claim our complete interest since it shows us the distortion, the sexual-symbolic disguise, and the mental overlay of the primitive sexual material, while the second dream actually attracts our interest only to the extent that it shows us the ways in which the dream work effects its characteristic distortion.

This approach also avoids the impression of arbitrariness associated, in the opinion of some readers, with my interpretive technique since it takes a given dream element sometimes in a positive and sometimes in a negative sense, sometimes historically (recollection), sometimes symbolically, and sometimes literally (Freud, 1909a, p. 245, footnote).

Indeed, the individual dream elements in every layer of mental life may have acquired one meaning or another. By placing these meanings in their natural place in a mental current (complex), they can be grasped with some degree of certainty.

In avoiding the temptation to attempt a theoretical acknowledgement, not yet even begun, of the importance of orgasmic dreams in light of the current case, already quite thoroughly discussed, I cannot avoid a theme that appears to have a universal meaning in dream life.

It would be no theoretical fiction, but completely in the realm of psychological possibility, if I were to imagine that the young woman had only dreamt the first dream and had then slept on undisturbed.

I could assume, in the sense of my previous discussions, that her erotic need, still awake during sleep, had been satisfied with the sexual gratification provided in the first dream in a disguised (inhibited) manner, and had calmed itself. But then I would hardly be in a position to understand the bluntly sexual sense of this dream in its full scope.

This suggests that many dreams to whose deepest meaning I am completely unable to penetrate may also be disguised orgasmic dreams. Under this interpretation, I would not only be approaching more closely the consistently sexual content of dream material, but would be in a position to recognise that in so many cases actual gratification does not occur because the infantile situation of gratification can only be reproduced in a disguised manner.

However, if the tension of the current libido is great enough to overcome completely all the mental inhibitions and resistances, then the infantile situation of gratification or the related fantasy, usually developed long ago in the unconscious, also enters the dream content and accompanies the form of infantile sexual gratification (masturbation) reactivated during sleep.[41]

Thus, I have already implicitly stated that every dream actually has the tendency and material to end in orgasm, with which, so to speak, the most complete wish-fulfilment would be attained.

The nightmare, though, should be understood as the polar opposite of the orgasmic dream. The nightmare, in fact, is only an unsuccessful attempt to present the disguised dream image that makes sleep possible.

In both cases, with the nightmare as with the orgasmic dream, the distortion of the dream is unsuccessful, while the presentation of the unconscious (of the sexual) is especially successful—indeed, too successful.

In the orgasmic dream, it breaks through pleasurably and undisguised in the form of infantile sexual gratification, accompanied by an unconscious ("perverse") fantasy.

In the nightmare, it can only establish itself in the opposite form of highly intensive sexual repression, that is, the ego reacts to it just as the neurotic does while awake: with anxiety.

Thus, nightmares and orgasmic dreams would be two unsuccessful, quasi-neurotic (and "perverse") outcomes of the dream work that regulates normal psychological life. They are the final members in a sequence within which human dream life plays out in the most diverse degrees and forms.

Against such a general application of the insights gained from an understanding of this dream, the objection could surely not be raised that the research subject is mentally abnormal. Such a claim would be based on the fact that the analysis has uncovered a psychosexual constitution and infantile experiences such as we are accustomed to finding in the analyses of neurotics.

But according to Freud (1909d, p. 160):

> One of the most valuable results of our psychoanalytic research is that the neuroses have no particular mental content specific to them alone. Rather, as Jung (1908) has expressed it, neurotics suffer from the same complexes we normals also struggle with. The only difference is that healthy persons succeed in overcoming these complexes without gross damage visible in practical life, while neurotics manage to overcome these complexes only at the price of costly substitute formations—in practical terms an unsuccessful result.

Yet "neurotics are human beings too, and should not be strictly set apart from other people; in childhood, they are not easily distinguished from those who remain healthy."

Our dreamer provides a shining proof of this claim. The proof results from the psychoanalytic illumination of a person who in practical life is not neurotic: she shows a tendency to neurosis and also a tendency to normalcy: both are evident in every direction.

With her early and rich sexual life, a situation not nearly as rare as was formerly believed (Freud, 1910a), and with her intensive repressions, she seems directly predisposed to neurosis.

Although she has thus far been able to maintain her active life, she has not completely overcome the transformations of her drives. She bears her normal neurosis, as do nearly all human beings. It has remained as the precipitate of her overflowing incestuous feelings. She has learned to accept it as her "fate" that again and again she must insert herself between father and mother (of the children in her care), and must soon leave the house due to disagreements with the mistress or sexual advances by the master.

In this sense, she has merely continued to play a childhood role, and when in her dream she produces a fantasy of the future, she is unable to give it any other content. One would be tempted to say that she lives out her neurosis in the normal erotic and social setting.

If, as should be permitted in a complete analysis, I now attempt to convey the meaning of this dream in a concise formula analogous to the manifest text, the briefest expression of the unconscious dream thoughts awakened on the eve of Saint Nicholas Day would be approximately as follows: "Under the inhibiting influences of my mother, my (sexual) life has arrived at its current ungratified state. If only she had died (instead of my father) (first dream), or if only I had been born as a boy (second dream), then I could have lived as myself (as in childhood)."

The two alternative wishes, which are not mutually exclusive, both take into account the dreamer's bisexual orientation,[50] and derive from the parent complex described above: the wish for the mother's death would enable her to be in love with her father undisturbed, and the much more intense wish to be a boy would allow a loving relationship with her mother, arising from homosexual feelings.

But, as it were, with a resigned reference to the impossibility of these wish-fulfilments, a counter-current in the dream portrays the actual development and life of the dreamer.

Indeed, if one observes the two portions of the dream as a whole, and reads this double dream backwards, in reversed order, it provides an overview of the inner developmental history of the dreamer's (sexual) life.[49]

First, we see the dreamer as an infant lying on her mother's breast. Then we see the important stages of her sexual (and social) development (pleasurable excretion, parent complex, masturbation, homosexual friendships, engagement, etc.) and her dissatisfaction with the outcome of these developments, which she seeks to correct through a fantasy of the future centred on her noble birth and distinguished marriage (within the scope of the parent complex).

But this projection of her infantile happiness into the future is still incapable of providing the actually desired gratification. Thus, in her wish fantasy, she places herself back into the blissful time when she was an infant nursing at her mother's breast—but this time as a boy.

Thus, as she consciously admits, her most fervent wish is to come back into the world as a man.

Endnotes

I. On the analysis

A.   Addenda to the dreams

1.   The conclusion that the dream expresses an infantile wish for the death of the mother, decisive for its further interpretation, is confirmed by the dreamer's subsequent statement that at the time of the queen's departure in the dream, the dreamer was wearing a close-fitting black dress with a white apron. This struck her as remarkable since she does not normally wear mourning and recalls only one such occasion, at the time of her father's death. From that time dates her open enmity with her mother, whom she would far rather have lost than her father, better loved in terms of her manifest feelings. On account of her mother, she was obliged to leave home.

As is characteristic of the determining influence of the unconscious life of thoughts, the dreamer, apparently independently of this long-forgotten dream, had just such a close-fitting black dress made for herself to wear during her most recent trip. When asked the reason for acquiring this ill-omened costume, she replied: "One never knows what will happen; at least one will be prepared."

1a.   Soon after receiving the pink nightgown, the young woman received a piece of white cloth as a gift from her mother, from which she had a "close-fitting" dress made—like the one in the dream. In the dream content, this gift from her mother is dyed, as it were, becoming a mourning costume for the death of her mother, while the white colour of innocence is transferred to the apron, which in the second dream acquires a sinful significance.

Later, in a comedy by Adolphe L'Arronge (*Hasemann's Daughters*), the dreamer remembered seeing a governess wearing a dress just like the one in the dream: black with a white apron—also the typical costume of a chambermaid. Black with white is worn especially by children as a sign of mourning (half-mourning), and in many areas lilac carries the same meaning.

2. As a later addendum, clearly betraying the incest fantasy, came a thought that had accompanied the announcement of the queen's departure in the dream. The dreamer thought to herself: "If she goes away, then I'll be alone with the king."

3. The young woman claimed to have had a similar feeling in the dream itself when the queen commanded her to lie on the floor: "The things she demands of me! I must prostrate myself like a Chinese person."

4. Addendum: "The queen said it was a forbidden room, and that only those to whom she grants permission may enter." That is, it is the mother who grants access to sexual pleasure. She actually forbade her daughter to associate with certain female friends so that she would not be "corrupted."

5. When I later pointed out to the dreamer the striking fact that her mother does not appear in the second dream, though it depicts the dreamer's childhood, she said she had indeed seen her in the second dream as well, and provided an additional dream fragment to be inserted at the point where she tells her friend she must first take the ears home before she can return to her. "I was in the yard at home: at first only the landlady's daughter-in-law was there, and then also the landlady herself. They were eating dumplings stuffed with cherries. I saw a dumpling that was broken open, and the cherries that were so black inside it. I was so surprised and happy that there were cherries already. The landlady and her daughter-in-law admired the ears of grain. They invited me to taste the dumplings, but I didn't want to. Rather, I threw the grains I had rubbed out with my fingers to the hens, who ate them. (Vague: the door was open and I wanted to go in to tell my mother I was back. I was surprised

that she had not heard me talking.) A third person was also standing there eating. I think this third person could have been my mother."

Given the confused nature of this hesitantly shared detail, we recognise, according to a dream regularity, an important piece of information from the dream thoughts. Crucially, it is confirmed that the mother's absence in the second dream is in fact tendentiously justified in the sense we have discussed. She cannot appear here clearly because with her presence all the inhibitions would return that disturb and hinder sexual pleasure. This is the reason why in the dream an unknown person is seen dimly and blurred. Only after resistance by conscious thought is overcome can this person be recognised as a possible personification of the mother. The blurred and vague character of this detail and the doubts about its accuracy are "offspring and instrument of mental resistance" (Freud, 1909a, p. 319), and the stubborn amnesia with regard to this scene must also be regarded as their work.

This portion of the dream, hazily seen, and remembered only with difficulty, reminds the dreamer of her strict mother, but also removes her at the same time, and it is significant that this scene is inserted before the act of sex. It betrays an oppressive sense of guilt in regard to the mother, and among its various sources the beating the dreamer received when she was fourteen gains a new meaning in this context. She was beaten because she had gone to a female friend's house rather than doing an errand for her mother, and had then lied about it. In the dream, she is to go to a friend's house again (to carry out the sex act), but then the sense of guilt arises, reminding her of the punishment to which she had to submit in reality (and also in the first dream), and admonishing her to go home first to tell her mother. Here, though, the tendency for wish-fulfilment obscures the appearance of the mother, who thus can neither approve nor punish the (sexual) plan of her daughter. A similar avoidance of the punishment is noted in an addendum to the first dream: the child, apparently a personification of the dreamer as a child, suddenly vanishes from the governess's side as she makes her way to the child's mother, who is ready to punish (cf. Endnote 25). The location mentioned in this addendum to the second dream also derives from the memory of a real beating scene. The young woman had actually once been struck by her mother in fun with a birch broom in the yard, and in the first dream too—though in the royal court (parents' home)—she is beaten with a birch switch. The mistress of the house where the dreamer's family were living when she visited some years before, and the woman's daughter-in-law—as memories of actual experience—are taken up into the dream content unaltered because the relationship of these two persons outside the family is to some extent a reflection of the dreamer's relationship to her mother. At the time of the dreamer's stay in her hometown, this daughter(-in-law) had fallen out with her mother(-in-law), and was on the point of leaving their shared home. Now our dreamer had also quarrelled with her mother and left the house. Based on this commonality, the identification in the dream can be made. Thus, while the conclusion of this scene portrays the fearful avoidance of punishment by the mother, the beginning portrays the defiance and rebellion of the grown young woman (daughter-in-law) toward her mother (mistress of the house). This addendum thus betrays—as does the leave-taking ceremony in the first dream—the juxtaposition of two opposite feelings toward the mother: a fearfully respectful, tender feeling and a defiantly mocking and hostile one. The identification with this daughter-in-law may express approximately the thought: "I am no longer afraid of you as in childhood, when I avoided punishment like a coward! If I don't like the way you treat me, I'll simply leave the house like this daughter-in-law. I am just as independent of you as she is of her mother-in-law." As to refusing the offered food, the dreamer later remembered a similar scene which took place during her last summer visit, when the mistress of the house offered her cherry pie to taste: she felt only disgust for it— seemingly without reason—and gave it to her mother to eat. Here in the dream, through reference to the expression "to eat cherries with some-one" [to get along well (Translator's Note)], an allusion is made to the young woman's strongly emphasised food complex, which in children often replaces the sexual complex (cf. Freud, 1908).

5a.   Early during her stays at home and also in unfamiliar surroundings, she even feels disgust for foods prepared well and in a sanitary manner, including those prepared by her mother, so that she often has to cook for herself at first. This strongly marked, almost neurotic, feeling of disgust is evidence of an originally highly pleasurable function of the oral zone, first in the enjoyable activity of nursing at her mother's breast, and later in making childish noises. This pleasurable function later experienced an intense repression constituted by disgust.

B.   Addenda to the material

6.   On being asked about the origin of the different coloured rooms, the dreamer said she had often thought about how she would decorate her rooms if she were married: one room would be green, a colour she was extremely fond of, the bedroom pink, etc. This thus relates to the young woman's fantasy about arrangements for her household in wedded life.

7.   The colours of the rooms are over-determined in many ways, for example, by the various colours of the parrots (pink parrot: bird) and also by the marriage fantasy (pink bedroom). In this connection, she also mentioned that, during her last stay at home, the bedroom (of her parents) with its pink bedspreads had made an especially good impression on her. As the decisive factor, though, she stressed the lasting impression made on her by the opera *Ariadne and Bluebeard* by Paul Dukas, a dramatic version of the fairy tale *Bluebeard*. The six permitted rooms were represented in various colours (red, blue, yellow, white, etc.), effectively contrasting with the shared lilac backdrop. Finally, the lilac colour reminded her of the cornflowers she used to pick in the summer amidst the yellow grain (yellow room), and also of the uniform of her fiancé, which bore a similar colour.

8.   The hotel fantasy we have identified is confirmed by a later statement about the identity of the "tutor," who had the features (beard) and build of a young high school teacher (tutor) who was an admirer of hers at one time. After a fairly long acquaintance, he wanted to invite her to dinner (locking up: private booth). She refused brusquely as she feared an invitation to a hotel. Later, she regretted that she had not declined more graciously. On the other hand, she had always had the impression that he was married, and that he thus had no serious intentions.

8a.   A later statement by the dreamer demonstrates the connection of the oleander-like trees with the hotel fantasy. They are described as being like those "that one sees in hotel entrances." In the dream, they stand before an entrance to the lilac room, which is thereby directly characterised as a hotel room.

9.   While cutting off the ears of grain she had thought to herself: "If they see me, they will lock me up." In the dream, she is to be locked up in the lilac room, which must relate to similar threats of punishment in childhood.

10.   During her walks last summer, just as she had done as a child, she had really torn off ears of grain and had been afraid someone would see her (anxiety in the dream) since tearing off the ears, especially of unripe grain, is not condoned by farmers. But this current affect achieves its full significance only through unconscious intensifications from the infantile sexual sphere. The connection of the infantile-erotic and the current feeling of guilt when tearing off ears of grain is brought about by the fact that in childhood she was repeatedly forbidden by her mother to engage in the "sinful tearing off of God's gifts."

10a.   It is not impossible that the "inverted" early ripening of the barley could have a homosexual meaning insofar as it expresses the fact that the dreamer was still associating with young women, whereas female friends who had also reached early sexual maturity were associating with young men. However, as if in justification of her choice, she mentioned the dangers of associating with men (child).

11.   The identification of the two young men in the second dream is completed by the comment that during their walk her fiancé, while crossing a bridge near the public baths, half-jokingly said that he felt like jumping into the water. He took off his coat halfway so that his shirt was partially visible. But according to a later comment, in the dream her young friend Z. was seen only in shirtsleeves. The dreamer had nothing to say about her innocent friendship in youth with Z. except that her aunt, with whom she lived after her mother remarried and before she departed from her hometown, had forbidden her to associate with him. His family name is partially identical (this is the nodal point) to the first name of her first fiancé, with whom things had not worked out well.

12.   Her fiancé had really stood a few paces ahead of her in great astonishment. But she continued (towards him) as if she did not know him. This, of course, led to their encounter.

12a.   Her emphasis on the fact that her fiancé "had not come closer," in connection with the especially emphasised "kiss among the ears of grain," makes probable a more intimate relationship with the fiancé—but of course, for obvious reasons, this could not be determined.

13.   During this unexpected meeting he had asked her: "Where are you coming from?" She had answered: "I was taking a walk," and had then asked: "Where are you coming from?" (the second young woman's question). "She also came here from Vienna" refers first of all to the visit of the

dreamer herself, but is also what the dreamer herself said about a female friend, and is furthermore what the dreamer's aunt said about a young woman who had previously been admired by H.

From this conversation with her fiancé also derive the conversations of the first dream. Thus the similar structure of the conversations in the two dreams is explained by their derivation from a common source. In conclusion to his initial remarks, reported above, her fiancé had said: "I only met you on my last day, and tomorrow I have to leave." "So," I said, "you're already leaving tomorrow?" "Yes, unfortunately I need to leave." This conversation, besides its literal meaning, also had the previously discussed unconscious meaning of incest (regret that the more beloved father had to die, and not the disturbing mother instead). This is clear from the appearance of these phrases in the dream content and from the affect of regretful surprise accompanying them. In reality, the young woman was relieved to hear the news of her fiancé's departure, though she probably put up a pretence of conventional regret.

14.   Like her fiancé, the king in the dream, whom she would have liked to marry, must "unfortunately go away" (death of the father). The identification of these two persons is further seen in the fact that the king in the dream, like the fiancé in reality (and friend Z., who represents him in the dream), is seen in shirtsleeves (while washing).

The identification of the dream king with the dreamer's brother is confirmed by her later comment on the dream thought that the young king was not at all suitable for the old queen: "He could sooner have been her son" (that is, the brother of the dreamer). Her affection for her father (incest fantasy) is transferred onto her brother and also onto her fiancé. Presumably, behind the rejecting comment of the king ("Pardon, this is not your room"), lies also the dreamer's disappointment over the naturally no longer so affectionate behaviour of her brother, whom she had seen while she was at home in the summer.

15.   As we have seen, figuring prominently in her unconscious dream thoughts is the fear that her mother will send no gift. Beyond the dreamer's personal feeling of guilt, this relates to a real reason. When she had left her hometown for the first time, her mother had given her a sum of money to cover expenses, and also, separately, 20 kroner as spending money. After her most recent visit, she had expected a similar gift. She took the absence of such a gift as a sign that her mother would

no longer be so generous toward her, and that she would probably not send the promised gift. For this disappointment too, connected with her departure (travel expenses), compensation is made in the dream. Just as the governess is taken into a Chinese lilac room as a reward, the chambermaid (reversed: the dreamer) receives 20 guldens from the queen before her departure—thus double the amount actually expected by the dreamer. Here, we note a partial identification of the dreamer with the chambermaid that has occurred through the hotel fantasy. (The black dress with the white apron, worn by the dreamer, is of course the typical attire of a chambermaid.) The chambermaid is to receive 20 kreuzers (for unlocking the doors). As suggested by this identification, the 20 kreuzers are intended, as it were, as a payment to the dreamer herself for love. The underlying common thought is the expectation of a reward for every demonstration of love (be it a reward from her mother or from a man), such as a child may be used to receiving.

16.   Here again, the ambitious-erotic fantasies of her waking life are relevant. One of these further determines the Chinese milieu. Recently, she had heard that there were Chinese men in Vienna who supposedly spared no cost to make the acquaintance of European ladies. She now developed the fantasy that she would marry one of them, or a Japanese man, or even a black man, as long as he had a high social rank (prince or king) and was very rich. Here again, we note the dreamer's trait, previously mentioned, of always expecting a reward for her love (in the broadest sense). Already in the manifest dream content, she is rewarded for obedience to her mother, and in the dream thoughts the wish arises that she be paid (20 kreuzers) for her love for a man (prostitution fantasy, hotel). She associates with her two female friends in the dream only because of their wealth, and in her daydreams, the wealthy and distinguished man dominates—who could even be Chinese. Just as this wish to marry a king ultimately derives from her father, the Chinese queen represents her mother in the dream (identification derived from the incest complex). In her fantasy, the dreamer had already adopted the persona of the Chinese queen so securely that she was already thinking about the (Chinese) décor for her rooms.

17.   A later comment reveals that the dreamer has been wishing for years to enter the service of a count. Consciously, though, she has never advanced to the fantasy of a position in the royal palace. Unconsciously, this fantasy is of infantile origin.

18. According to a comment by the dreamer, the situation in the first dream, and the Chinese milieu, derive from the lasting impression of the well-known operetta *The Geisha* [lyrics by Harry Greenbank, musical score by Sidney Jones (Translator's Note)], in which a similar scene occurs. The owner of the teahouse greets the police prefect by kneeling before him. The prefect, though, desires a more deferential act of submission. With his fan, he strikes the Chinese man on his bald pate, behind which dangles a long queue. Cringing, he lies down flat on the floor, almost touching it with his nose. Thus, this scene from *The Geisha* is the historical model of the greeting ceremony in the dream. (Cf. the dream thought: "I must prostrate myself like a Chinese person.")

19. The queen (mother) says that the tutor may only enter the forbidden room when the dreamer has left it. Thus, she does not allow the two of them to be alone together in the room. In reality, whenever the dreamer was visited by young people, her mother was always suspicious, much to the irritation of her daughter. This also relates to a visit to a doctor in the previous summer: the "tutor" has the doctor's facial features and blue-black goatee (*Bluebeard*). Ultimately, the dreamer's affective retrospection about her mother's not so unreasonable caution probably derives from the fact that the child cannot forgive the mother for disturbing the erotic relationship with the father, with whom the child is never "left alone" by the mother (death wish). In the structure of the scene of locking the room, beyond infantile bathroom memories, a preconscious memory of the dreamer certainly contributed as well: when she feared the approaches of one of the young male occupants of a home where she had once worked, she would lock herself up in her room (cf. Freud, 1905, p. 58). This unlocking and locking also reminded the dreamer of a scene during the past summer: after a walk with her former fiancé, she arrived home late, in his company. She found her mother already waiting for her, lurking behind the door. Her mother unlocked the door, let her daughter in, and then locked the door again. Listening to her mother's reproaches, she thought ironically: "You're standing there unlocking and locking the door like a concierge." Here, the 20 "kreuzer" fee for unlocking the door acquires another ironic meaning. In this identification with the chambermaid—the concierge to whom one gives 20 kreuzers—there is a disparagement of the mother corresponding approximately to the dream thought: "I won't stop at 20 kreuzers (travel expenses). I'll give you 20 kreuzer extra, as a woman of that

type would receive." One notices, incidentally, the similar word structures: *Hausmeister—Hofmeister* (concierge–steward), *Frauenzimmer—Stubenmädchen* (woman/woman's room—chambermaid), *Mannsbilder* (men/images of men). The word *Haus-Frau* (mistress of the house) can be constructed with *Haus* from the first set and *Frau* from the second set. In dreams, these primitive (infantile) processes of linguistic construction are reactivated (cf. *lila* and *lulu*, Endnote 25).

II. On symbolism

20. "Cultural historians point out that the oldest historical sculptures follow a similar principle [*as in the interpretation of dreams*]: the status of the persons represented is expressed by the size of their depiction in the sculpture ... To achieve the same purpose, a Roman sculpture employs finer means. The figure of the emperor is placed centrally, standing erect, with special attention paid to the presentation of his form. His enemies lie at his feet, but he no longer appears as a giant among midgets. Meanwhile, in our culture, the bow of a person of lower status before a person of higher status is an echo of this old representational principle" (Freud, 1909a, p. 369).

21. Concerning the bird as a phallic symbol, cf. Maeder (1906) and Seligmann (1910), especially on the concept of the winged phallus. See also Freud (1910b).

22. The interpretation of these fairy tales in the sense of masturbation is evinced in their all too clear symbolic guise. In one tale [*A Child of Saint Mary*], the girl's finger acquires a golden colour after she touches the heavenly fire in the forbidden room. Thus, the Virgin Mary realises that the child has sinned. In *Fitcher's Bird*, in addition to the key, the girl receives an egg. When she enters the forbidden room, it acquires a bloody colour, betraying the sinner. It should also be mentioned that through her activities with children, the dreamer is very familiar with these fairy tales, yet only *Bluebeard* occurred to her spontaneously. Sexual symbols found in dreams, identical to those found in fairy tales, include the bird, egg, key, etc. These thus derive not from conscious memories, but from the human collective unconscious.

23. Besides the entire connection of complexes, this interpretation is supported by the meaning of the apron, which in terms of content relates

closely to the ears of grain. In the deepest layer of the dream, it is employed in the sense of folk superstition (raising the apron: unfaithfulness). It is also employed in the sense of language (skirt-chaser), and in the archaic sense of a covering (primitive clothing, figleaf, loincloth). Finally, it appears as a symbol of the female genitals. A relevant preconscious memory leads to a bad joke she permitted herself during the time when she first had a fiancé, in Vienna. To one of her numerous and very insistent admirers, she sent a letter, addressed to his office, with the notation "To Herr Skirt Chaser." Indeed, she dissolved her first engagement because her fiancé turned out to be a skirt-chaser.

23a. The deepest connection of this apron symbolism is illuminated by the homosexual sense of the dream, in which the dreamer herself appears as a "skirt-chaser." On this masculine role, cf. Adler (1910).

24. The analogical relationship between rain and urine is familiar in myth, legend, folk belief, and language. Ehrenreich (1910, p. 140) comments concerning rain that remarkably often it is conceived as the excretion of a celestial being (urine, sweat, saliva). According to a legend related by Boas (1895, p. 174), the oceans and rivers were created through the urination of a human being. In another legend (1895, p. 238), a great river is created when a woman urinates. In support of the folk-psychological basis of the symbolism in the dream under discussion, where urine is symbolised by rain, Goldziher indicates that the name of the Arab god of storm and rain, Kuzah, is etymologically derived from the word referring to urination; this verb applies especially to the urination of animals: "Here, in myth, rain is conceived as urination, which will not sound outlandish to those familiar with the phraseology of myth. This fact motivates us to connect Hebrew *bul* 'rain, rainy month' with Arabic *bala, jabulu* 'urination'" (1876, p. 89). It should also be noted, finally, that in many German-speaking areas, among certain social classes, rain and urination are referred to with the same word, *schiffen*, and that this symbolism is also found in many ambiguous jokes.

25. With regard to certain linguistic associations (e.g. *urination, ruination*), the suspicion cannot be completely eliminated that the word *lila* (lilac), so important in the dream, is related through the reactivation of infantile wordplay to the child's word *lulu*, commonly used to designate urination. For a long time, the dreamer used this word and no other in

this sense. When she was once told by an employer to take the child *wischerin*, she did not understand the meaning of the term, and thus felt highly embarrassed. An addendum to the first dream is noticeably reminiscent of this scene: she takes the child by the hand and enters the bathroom (housebroken) as she makes her way to the queen. Given the urine remaining there, the room's yellow colour no longer seems arbitrary. The child then disappears suddenly, and she has the impression that the chambermaid, who of course cleans the rooms (hotel), has taken it away. It is clear that in this disappearance, the child—a personification of the infantile dreamer herself before she was toilet-trained—escapes punishment by the mother. On the other hand, it seems that the child is disappearing to the bathroom (the chambermaid takes the child away just as the dreamer should have done with the child in her care), for the next scene is of course the lilac (*lulu*) room. Only one person at a time may enter this room, which must be continually locked and unlocked. In the context of this bathroom fantasy, which may be connected with the masturbation complex, consider how the king is surprised in the pink room while making his toilet (bathroom).

26.   Winckelmann (1791) believes that the words *kepos* "garden," *leimo* "meadow," and *pedion* "field" have a completely different sense: they were humorously used in reference to the female genitals. Indeed, Aphrodite, goddess of love, was said to have oversight over gardens, meadows, and fields.

27.   Lying on the earth doubtless also has a symbolic meaning, and one need only recall individual and particularly obvious applications of this symbol, common throughout antiquity, to understand its meaning in the dream under discussion. Julius Caesar is said to have dreamt of sexual intercourse with his mother, and this was taken by dream interpreters as a good omen for conquering the world (Mother Earth). Equally well known is the oracular prediction given to the Tarquins stating that the first among them to kiss his own mother (*osculum matri tulerit*) would become the ruler of Rome. Brutus interpreted this as a reference to Mother Earth: *terram osculo contigit, scilicet quod ea communis mater omnium mortalium esset* [he kissed the earth since she is the common mother of all mortals (Translator's Note)] (Livy I: 56). The concept of Mother Earth is found not only among Indo-Europeans (Indic peoples,

Greeks, Germanic peoples), but also among the Native Americans, who go so far as to call her "the horizontally lying woman" (Ehrenreich, 1910). For earth symbolism, cf. also Aigremont, 1909.

This (unconscious) symbolic concept also plays a role in neurosis. Freud has recently interpreted the anxiety attack which overcame a patient who was working in the garden (occupational therapy) when the sun shone on him. According to the patient's own words, utilised by Freud in his interpretation, he was afraid of the Sun Father, who was watching him and had surprised him while he was working on Mother Earth. The ethnological counterpart of this concept is found among the Native Americans, whose resistance to the culture of ploughing is explained by Ehrenreich (1910) as a reluctance to injure the skin of Mother Earth.

The dream under discussion includes the phrase "the sun was shining," but I will not attempt to decide whether or not this phrase has a similar meaning. The core motivation for this comment is the fact that on the day of the walk, the sun was brightly shining.

28. With the help of "Chinese" sexual symbolism, another meaning of the lilac colour becomes comprehensible. In reality, the young woman is very fond of this colour. Whatever has a lilac colour is Chinese (in the dream)—bisexual—like the room. Just as lilac is a mixed colour, for the dreamer all things Chinese signify the bisexual realm. She readily admits that her interest in all things Chinese derives from the "sexually mixed" impression the Chinese make on her. The bird may also owe its stylish lilac colouring to the fact that in many bird species, males and females cannot easily be distinguished. When there is a distinction, the male usually possesses striking tail feathers. This "long tail" corresponds to the long and noticeable queue worn by the Chinese. In the dream, this is replaced by the long train of the Chinese gown. The bird that flies in from behind is reminiscent of the confusion between the two pink rooms, which from the outside (backwards) look the same, and the confusion in identifying the king, who seen from behind cannot be recognised as a man. In addition to this difficulty in determining gender, as a child, and to some extent today, the dreamer has had difficulty understanding the procreative processes of chickens. In this species, too, males are also distinguished from females by striking tail feathers.

III. On theory

29. "All dreams on the same night belong, according to their content, to the same whole. Their division into various parts, their grouping and number—all of this is meaningful and can be conceived as information from the latent dream thoughts" (Freud, 1909a).

30. "This force seeks to form something like a daydream from the material offered. When such a daydream has already been formed in connection with the dream thoughts, then this factor of the dream work will appropriate it and work to bring it into the dream content" (Freud, 1909a). In the current case, this is highly successful since most of the unconscious material that does not fit the content of the daydreams can be directed to the second dream. The young woman admits that she is a passionate and tireless daydreamer.

31. "It is worth emphasising that through the opposing result of the 'secondary elaboration,' which thus offers a particularly absurd dream façade, the dream work also succeeds in avoiding the conscious dreamer's conscious criticism, expressed in the judgement that the dream is complete nonsense, etc." (Freud, 1909a, p. 6).

32. One recognises here how the recent fantasies about Saint Nicholas Day, which directly trigger the first dream, lead to the superficial façade of the second dream, given the reproachful recollection of the inappropriate departure in the summer, connected with them. "The dream can select its material from any time in life, provided that a string of thoughts reaches from the experiences of the daydream (the 'recent' impressions) to these earlier experiences" (Freud, 1909a, p. 118). "The source stimulating the dream need not always be a recent event. The stimulus of the dream may be an inner process, which has as it were become recent through the work of thought during the day" (1909a, p. 127).

33. Equally reliable for the identification of deeper connections are the superficial associations arising from the individual wit and acumen of the dreamer. In the dream under discussion, for example, *Abreissen* "tearing off" (of the ears of grain) and *Abreisen* "travelling away" (of the queen, and actually of the dreamer) are similar not only in sound. Rather, *Abreissen* "tearing off" (of the ears of grain) leads to a deeper association with the departure of the dreamer, who was indeed "torn away" from her mother (without a farewell) due to the limitations on the dreamer's

(sexual) freedom (tearing off the ears of grain; prohibition)—limitations perceived as oppressive.

It is furthermore characteristic of the subtlety of dream structure that there is mention both of cutting off the ears and tearing off the ears. Tearing off or tearing out applies to the ears and symbolises masturbation, while cutting off is associated with the dreamer's honour, which represents the moral side of the complex. In *The Interpretation of Dreams* (Freud, 1909a, p. 134), the same example (*reisen, reissen*) is utilised to demonstrate how closely the child, still unsure of the use of language, must attend to such similar sounds.

34. In the course of the interpretation, it has often been necessary—too often, as critical readers will opine—to identify various persons appearing in the dream with the dreamer herself in order to achieve a deeper understanding of the dream thoughts. Some readers may be disturbed that in our analytical work almost none of the dream figures has been spared this reduction to the dreamer herself. To these readers, it should be directly stated that one of the most obvious prerequisites of dream psychology is of course the insight that all the persons appearing in the dream represent a part of the dreamer's own individuality, of the personal mental life of the dreamer. This recognition in no way contradicts the fact that in the dream, these persons can also reproduce a portion of meaning from waking life. Indeed, we are not offended when, in a historical drama, we see the personifications of real individuals endowed with the feelings and words of the playwright.

35. It should be pointed out that such a hypothetical acceptance of the explanation of unconscious mental processes can be seen as the complete and unreserved recognition of its accuracy.

36. The shifting of such embarrassing memories onto siblings seems typical (cf. Freud, 1905, p. 49 and p. 64).

37. This scene, experienced twice, in which the vain young men observe themselves in the mirror, seems to account for the fact that the king in the dream observes himself twice in the mirror (both in the washroom and in the yellow room, before his departure).

37a. It would be tempting to derive all the repetitions, multiplications (doublings), and stereotypes in the dream from the sexual gratification that is repeatedly sought and finally achieved several times.

38. Cf. the comment in Freud (1910a), which states that actively inverted women very often possess the physical and mental characteristics of men. In our dreamer's case, there is no physical sign of masculinity, but she does show mental traits which must be designated as masculine. Her tendency to inversion must nevertheless be regarded as latent (unconscious, repressed). On being asked, she says: "[I] like to look at pictures of women," but she indicates that in reality she finds few women appealing in person. For many years, she has had no female friends. She prefers to associate with young men in relationships characterised by friendship and camaraderie. This looks completely heterosexual, but to perceptive persons, it again reveals her tendency to inversion.

39. In this comment too, her tendency to inversion breaks through once again.

40. The dreamer's preference for masculine clothing mainly involves putting on men's caps, especially those of uniforms. In the previous summer, she tried on the military caps of her previous fiancé, her brother, and her cousin. She believes that this "cap fetish" derives from the fact that, as a small child, she always waited with impatience for her father's return home so that she could put on his civil service cap. From this, we must conclude that she displays a form of "masculinity" already evinced early in her life, and expressed in her wishes for identification with her father. Such an identification is conceivable only based on intense love for the corresponding person. On the other hand, this identification with her father apparently has the sense of playing his (masculine) role with respect to her mother, which again presupposes an erotic inclination toward her. We must therefore think of the dreamer as originally very much in love with both parents. This was later followed by a one-sided repression of her love for her mother, leading to an orientation characterised by the feminine Oedipus complex. If one wonders which parent is preferred, she is actually a child who would solve the issue by being in love with both of them. Here, we see the original expression of her bisexual orientation.

41. This is especially clear in orgasmic dreams of sexual intercourse with the mother, discussed by Freud in detail as typical dreams (1909a, p. 175 ff.). In this context, the sex act as such is autoerotic (masturbatory), as is the case with orgasmic dreams in general, and is

accompanied by the boyhood masturbation fantasy, now unconscious, featuring the sex act with the mother as its content.

42. The young woman demonstrates an "anal character," seldom clearly expressed, with an especially strongly emphasised cleanliness complex (public baths, pink wash basin). Cf. Freud (1909e).

42a. The anal eroticism that originally underlay her anal character is revealed by coprophilic tendencies suggested in the dream content, but also by a more distant association. In the dream, there is a clear emphasis on the fact that with her switch the mother strikes the child in the face: such punishments are generally reserved for the opposite part of the body. Since Rousseau's famous confession, whipping the buttocks has been acknowledged as a source of exquisitely (anal) erotic gratification. This clarifies the fact that in the multiply reversed dream content, this body part too is represented by its opposite: this reversal results from the repression of masochistic-anal sensations of pleasure. However, the dreamer is also familiar with the Chinese system of corporal punishment, which prescribes whipping the face.

43. Sadger (1910) has noted the anal erotic source, not uncommon among older women, of lifting up their skirts—no less often exhibitionistically conditioned. In one of his cases, fear of wetting the clothes plays a role.

44. Freud (1909e) has already indicated the connection between excessive, "burning" ambition, revealed in the fantasy life of our dreamer, and earlier bed-wetting. This ambitiousness among bed-wetters apparently derives from the tendency to compensate for the constantly feared criticisms over this childhood fault by seeking honour for extraordinary achievements.

45. It is obviously not this event that brought about the transformation of her cruelty into pity. Rather, the "increase in repression at puberty" (Freud, 1910a, p. 26), which eliminated the dreamer's presumably extremely pronounced masculine traits, was already underway; even the unsuccessful slaughter of the chicken was a sign of this transformation.

45a. These transformational processes may explain the fact that the beating is the only event from this time remaining in the young woman's lasting memory.

46. She even admits to having once raised her hand in anger to strike her mother. To the sadistic complex belongs also the dreamer's recollection

that as a child she took the sexual activity of chickens as fighting (something very typical), and the fact that she arrived at her masturbatory object gratification (playing "father and mother") through wrestling. (Cf. Freud's mention of the "sadistic conception of coitus.") Also, the powerful effect of the opera *Ariadne and Bluebeard* and of the submission scene from *The Geisha* is based on sadistic-masochistic drive impulses. On the unification of both of these possibilities for gratification in the same person, cf. Rank, 1907.

The predilection of dreams for the use of scenes really seen on stage (cf. also the governess in *Hasemann's Daughters*, Endnote 1a) in the depiction of corresponding dream thoughts is explained by the unique characteristics of the task facing the dreamer, and by the limited means of representation available. The need for a clear and meaningful representation of the dream thoughts is seen also in the return to the originally very concrete, physical interpretation of certain conceptions which later remain only as idiomatic expressions, "to eat cherries with someone" [to get along well (Translator's Note)], or "to rub something under someone's nose" [to reproach someone (Translator's Note)], etc.

47.   After persistent questioning, the dreamer admitted to having awakened from the dream lying on her stomach. This circumstance should certainly not be interpreted according to the theory of bodily stimulation, as if the young woman simply ended up on her stomach by chance and as if the stimulation of the external genitalia possibly brought about by this position had produced the orgasm and the corresponding dream image. The correct conception, built on the foundation of a psychological dream analysis, is rather the assumption of an original libidinous excitation as a result of which the young woman enters the infantile masturbatory position in a state of sleep—a position which also produces the dream images conditioned by infantile factors.

48.   Freud has also noted the cultural-historical significance of this layering of mental life. As an especially instructive folk-psychological example of this type, consider the two previously mentioned fairy tales (Grimm & Grimm, 1885)—*A Child of Saint Mary* and *Fitcher's Bird*—which in terms of their sexual-symbolic disguise versus clarity stand in a relationship similar to that of the two portions of the dream under discussion. This explains the characteristic comment of the young woman—whose dreams are very frequent, clear, and lively—that she has dreams of

precisely two types: beautiful, poetic, and usually "flowery" ones like the first one, and then "dreams of the second type." Based on our analysis, we can explain this apparent opposition in her dream life by stating that she, like other women too, actually produces only one kind of dream— bluntly sexual ones—sometimes well disguised and sometimes less so. Freud has repeatedly emphasised (1909a, p. 129 and p. 2) that especially innocent dreams conceal especially offensive material.

49.   According to Freud, this is a frequent type—the so-called "biographical dreams."

50.   From an analysis of a great many dreams of adults, one gains the impression that many of them, especially richly elaborated ones, cannot be fully explained with a meaning relating to the opposite sex. Rather, like the hysterical symptom, such dreams often derive their deepest significance from same-sex emotional life, and are thus bisexual. But here, the limitation applies which Freud makes for the hysterical symptom as well: the claim does not apply to all the dreams of a single person, and cannot be expected of every dream. Here, rather, besides numerous "bisexual" dreams, homosexual impulses often enough are expressed separately in a dream dedicated especially to them.

References

Adler, Alfred (1910). Der psychische Hermaphroditismus im Leben und in der Neurose [Mental hermaphroditism in life and in neurosis]. *Fortschritte der Medizin*, no. 16.

Aigremont, Siegmar, Baron von Gallera (1909). *Fuss- und Schuh-Symbolik und -Erotik* [Foot and shoe symbolism and eroticism]. Leipzig: Deutsche Verlags-Aktien-Gesellschaft.

Boas, Franz (1895). *Indianische Sagen von der nordpacifischen Küste Amerikas* [Indian legends of the North Pacific coast of America]. Berlin: Asher.

Ehrenreich, Paul (1910). *Die allgemeine Mythologie und ihre ethnologischen Grundlagen* [General mythology and its ethnological bases]. Leipzig: Hinrich'sche Buchhandlung.

Freud, Sigmund (1900). *Die Traumdeutung* [The interpretation of dreams]. Vienna: Deuticke.

Freud, Sigmund (1905). *Bruchstück einer Hysterie-Analyse* [Fragment of an analysis of hysteria]. In Freud 1909d.

Freud, Sigmund (1907). Der Wahn und die Träume in W. Jensens *Gradiva* [Delusion and dreams in W. Jensen's *Gradiva*]. *Schriften zur Angewandten Seelenkunde*, no. 1.

Freud, Sigmund (1908). Über infantile Sexualtheorien [On infantile sexual theories]. In *Gesammelte Schriften* [Collected writings], vol. 5. Vienna: Internationaler Psychoanalytischer Verlag, 1925.

Freud, Sigmund (1909a). *Die Traumdeutung* [The interpretation of dreams]. Vienna: Deuticke (2nd edn.).

Freud, Sigmund (1909b). Analyse der Phobie eines fünfjährigen Knaben [Analysis of the phobia of a five-year-old boy]. *Jahrbuch für psychoanalytische und psychopathologische Forschungen*, no. 1.

Freud, Sigmund (1909c). Bemerkungen über einen Fall von Zwangsneurose [Comments on a case of obsessional neurosis]. *Jahrbuch für psychoanalytische und psychopathologische Forschungen*, no. 1.

Freud, Sigmund (1909d). *Sammlung kleiner Schriften zur Neurosenlehre* [Collected lesser writings on the study of neurosis]. Vienna: Deuticke (2nd edn.).

Freud, Sigmund (1909e). *Charakter und Analerotik* [Character and anal eroticism]. In Freud, 1909d.

Freud, Sigmund (1910a). *Drei Abhandlungen zur Sexualtheorie* [Three essays on the theory of sexuality]. Vienna: Deuticke.

Freud, Sigmund (1910b). *Eine Kindheitserinnerung des Leonardo da Vinci* [A childhood memory of Leonardo da Vinci]. Vienna: Deuticke.

Goethe, J. W. V. (1837). *Faust*. Trans. B. Taylor. Boston: James R. Osgood, 1871.

Goldziher, Ignác (1876). *Der Mythos bei den Hebräern und seine geschichtliche Entwickelung* [Myth among the Hebrews and its historical development]. Leipzig: Brockhaus.

Grimm, Jacob, & Wilhelm (1885). *Kinder- und Hausmärchen* [Folktales for children and for the home]. Berlin: Dümmler.

Jung, Carl (1908). *Der Inhalt der Psychose* [The content of psychosis]. Leipzig: Deuticke.

Jung, Carl (1909). Die Bedeutung des Vaters für das Schicksal des Einzelnen [The significance of the father in the destiny of the individual]. *Jahrbuch für psychoanalytische und psychopathologische Forschungen*, no. 1.

Maeder, Alphonse (1906). Essai d'interprétation de quelques rêves [Essay on the interpretation of some dreams]. *Archives de Psychologie*, no. 6, 24.

Rank, Otto (1907). *Der Künstler: Ansätze zu einer Sexualpsychologie* [The artist: Approaches to a sexual psychology]. Vienna: Heller.

Rank, Otto (1909). *Der Mythos von der Geburt des Helden* [The myth of the birth of the hero]. Leipzig: Deuticke.

Riklin, Franz (1908). Wunscherfüllung und Symbolik im Märchen [Wish fulfilment and symbolism in fairy tales]. *Schriften zur Angewandten Seelenkunde*, no. 2.

Sadger, Isidor (1910). Analerotik und Analcharakter [Anal eroticism and anal character]. *Die Heilkunde*, no. 2, 43–46.

Seligmann, Siegfried (1910). *Der böse Blick und Verwandtes* [The evil eye and related material]. Berlin: Barsdorf.

Stekel, Wilhelm (1908a). Die Symbolik des Märchens [The symbolism of fairy tales]. *Die Zeit, Feuilleton*.

Stekel, Wilhelm (1908b). *Nervöse Angstzustände und ihre Behandlung* [Nervous states of anxiety and their treatment]. Berlin: Urban and Schwarzenberg.

Stekel, Wilhelm (1909). *Beiträge zur Traumdeutung* [Contributions to the interpretation of dreams]. *Jahrbuch für psychoanalytische und psychopathologische Forschungen*, no. 1.

Winckelmann, Johann Joachim (1791). *Alte Denkmäler der Kunst* [History of the art of antiquity]. Berlin: Schone.

Index